KT-198-355

C333996722

Business for Bohemians

By the same author

How to be Idle

How to be Free

The Book of Idle Pleasures (*with Dan Kieran*)

The Idle Parent

Brave Old World

The Ukulele Handbook
(*with Gavin Pretor-Pinney*)

Business for Bohemians

Live Well, Make Money

TOM HODGKINSON

PORTFOLIO
PENGUIN

For my mother

PORTFOLIO PENGUIN

UK | USA | Canada | Ireland | Australia
India | New Zealand | South Africa

Portfolio Penguin is part of the Penguin Random House group of companies
whose addresses can be found at global.penguinrandomhouse.com.

First published 2016
001

Copyright © Tom Hodgkinson, 2016

The moral right of the author has been asserted

May we convey our sincerest gratitude to Modern Toss for their most gracious
permission to use the cartoon on page 110 in exchange for two copies of the finished
book (which they will probably sell on eBay, slightly cheaper than the cover price).
Contact info@moderntoss.com if you're interested.

Set in 12.5/14.75 pt Garamond MT Std
Typeset by Jouve (UK), Milton Keynes
Printed in Great Britain by Clays Ltd, St Ives plc

A CIP catalogue record for this book is available from the British Library

ISBN: 978−0−241−24479−1

www.greenpenguin.co.uk

MIX
Paper from
responsible sources
FSC
www.fsc.org   FSC® C018179

Penguin Random House is committed to a
sustainable future for our business, our readers
and our planet. This book is made from Forest
Stewardship Council® certified paper.

Contents

CONTENTS

Introduction

April 2016

Artists, writers, musicians and creative types in general tend to have a horror of the mechanics of business. Terms like 'cashflow forecasts', 'spreadsheets' and 'VAT returns' stir up feelings of, at best, boredom, and at worst, pure terror. We artists would like to be free of the tawdry world of commerce. We want to lie about on a richly embroidered ottoman smoking a hookah pipe while discussing Oscar Wilde. We want to be free. We want to get loaded. We don't see ourselves evaluating a marketing strategy and spending an away-day in an airless office with a flip chart doing a SWOT analysis, still less carrying out performance reviews, firing staff and producing mission statements.

Can you really be a bohemian in business? Surely the bohemian – the freedom-seeker, the contemplative soul, the poet, the philosopher – floats above the everyday world of commerce and competition, all that vulgar shouting, and bustling, and shoving, forever trying to make your voice heard above the din?

Well, yes. It would be nice to be free of vulgar trade. But most of us need to earn some sort of income. So we bohemians decide that rather than working for the Man, we should become freelancers, sole traders, entrepreneurs. We want to create something useful or beautiful or both and sell it. This is a noble and wonderful goal. I can think of nothing better.

And this is undeniably the way the world is heading. The success of start-ups such as Uber, Airbnb and sell-your-wares website Etsy is a sure sign that people everywhere are aspiring to a greater degree of control over their working day. They aspire to freedom. And Uber, Airbnb and Etsy have profited handsomely from this trend.

Bohemianism, of course, is all about freedom, and so is running a business.

But it ain't easy. The idea that you can knit a tea cosy, put it up for sale on a website, tweet about it, watch the orders come flooding in and quit your job is pure fantasy. Making stuff is easy. Selling it is not.

And if you're not very careful, your creative business, the very thing which you hoped would lead to liberty and riches, will instead trap you in a hell of hard-working poverty. I know, I've been there. Read this book, and maybe you'll manage to avoid making the mistakes I made.

What I aim to do here is to teach the rudiments of small business and help you to make a living doing something you enjoy. When you start up on your own, you find that every obstacle conceivable is hurled in your path. It's hard work. Harder work than you can imagine. And for someone who teaches people to be idle, this was a little tricky for me to get my head around.

Throughout the noughties, I was a full-time writer. But towards the end of the decade, the world of publishing and journalism began to look decidedly ropey. The money did not seem to be there any more. So I decided to go into business. And that has been decidedly tougher.

In March 2011, my partner and I opened a combined coffeehouse, bookshop and events venue in London called the Idler Academy of Philosophy, Husbandry and Merriment. Nice idea. Let's sit around in a bookshop like Nancy Mitford at Heywood Hill and run jolly little salons for the wits of the day. Erm, it wasn't quite like that, I'm afraid.

I was thrown from a four-hour workday writing books to a fourteen-hour day serving customers, ordering books, trying to do journalism, sending weekly newsletters stressing about dirty lavatories and moving furniture around for events. For two years, I woke every morning at five thirty in a blind panic and lay in bed worrying for two hours before crawling to the laptop in my pyjamas.

Having been a guru of laid-back living, I found I had morphed into a horrific combination of David Brent and Basil Fawlty. Making a coffee for a customer filled me with fear and humiliation. I was branded a 'pretentious lunatic' in an online review a week after opening by an angry punter. I proved to be a terrible boss, alternating between chumminess and rage. I upbraided staff for being late and was accused by one of them of 'micro-managing', a term I had never heard before.

We found that, while money came into the business and went out again, we owners – my partner Victoria and me – were the only people not seeing any of it. Staff, suppliers, tutors, landlord, council, bank, HMRC: all had to be paid before us. At times, it is easy to think that you are working only for the banks and the landlord.

Well, this is reality. If you want freedom, then you have to take responsibility, and that means opening the boring post and dealing with it; it means filing your VAT return on time.

I have also learned that business is a skill, like carpentry. It must be studied and practised. You will make many mistakes. And it may take you many years to become competent at it. In the old days, an apprenticeship lasted seven years, and that is probably about right for business, too.

My own story is briefly this: I have been job-free since 1997. I spent the nineties running around London. I started my own magazine, the *Idler*, aimed at people who would really rather not have a job. I wrote a piece in the *Guardian* called 'Why I Don't Want a Job', and the following week they offered me one. I become head of editorial development, alongside my friend and co-worker Gav. After three years, we quit to start our own creative agency. Our clients included Channel 4 and Sony PlayStation. We produced magazines and ads to help these brands, and within a couple of years we were turning over £250,000, most of which went straight into our pockets, as we had modest overheads.

We spent almost every evening in the Spread Eagle pub in Camden Town, the nearest one to our office. One of my drinking pals was John Moore, a charismatic musician who had played drums in the Jesus and Mary Chain. One evening, the talk turned to John's plans to import absinthe from the Czech Republic. We fantasized about starting our own business to do just that. Two years later, it actually happened: we kicked off the UK absinthe boom with the slogan 'Tonight we're going to party like it's 1899.' In the first year, I took home a dividend of £20,000, which was not bad. I soon got bored, though, and sold my share back to our business partner.

Then I got bored of running a creative agency. I woke up one morning and decided to quit and write books instead. My partner and I moved out of London. We rented a remote farmhouse and stayed there for ten years. I wrote five books, including *How to be Idle*, which sold in twenty countries around the world, from China to Korea, Finland to Estonia. I chopped logs in the afternoon, grew vegetables, kept pigs and continued to edit the *Idler*. It was a great life. The books did pretty well. Two became best-sellers, and I still get nice cheques every few months from foreign and UK sales.

In 2000, Victoria and I launched a new festival project, the Idler Academy. We took over a tent at the Port Eliot Festival and ran a programme of classes, talks and medieval music performances. Our first lesson was called 'How to sew on a button properly' and was given by a Savile Row tailor.

This was great fun. On holiday over the summer, our well-to-do friend Robin Birley, who runs London's most luxuriously appointed private club, put the idea into our heads of starting a full-time *Idler* hangout in London.

Suddenly, we found ourselves remortgaging, borrowing money from the bank and taking out a lease on a shop in a quiet corner of Notting Hill. We ran this for five years and built up what you might call a strong events business.

But wow, it was tough. This was the real thing. We really did not have a clue what we were doing. We had every problem you can think of: angry staff, angry Inland Revenue, negative cashflow, naysayers, new competitors – the usual stuff. We managed to increase our turnover from £150,000 in the first year to £220,000 in the fifth year, and also made a small profit.

Following a conversation with a friend of mine at Etsy, we decided to produce two online versions of our courses. We hired a filmmaker and filmed six lectures on ancient philosophy – the Stoics, the Epicureans and the rest – with our philosophy teacher, Mark Vernon. We bundled them up with a few pages of nicely designed notes and access to an 'Ask the teacher' forum. We put them on sale and sold one hundred in a day.

Our online courses are beautiful and useful things which people love. The idea attracted our first angel investor, and we went on to produce a series of sixteen quirky, funny and very English courses with top experts in their fields. Every course is now in profit.

Then we embarked on a fund-raising campaign to expand our digital offering. We also decided to stop renting a shop, due to a realization that it is in the wrong location – and to save a gigantic overhead.

This book is the fruit of five years' experience at the frontline of running an education, retail and publishing business, and of twenty years of self-employment.

My mantra has always been 'Just keep going', despite feeling like giving up every other day, because I know that we're doing something that brings meaning and purpose to people's lives. Our customers, our fans, our community, our readers – love what we do. I enjoy it. And those are the three words I hear again and again among entrepreneurs: just keep going.

No other path offers the same sort of freedom. It's not about making a vast fortune and being some sort of amoral hedge-fund manager who is interested only in money. It is about creating something that improves the world, is fun to do and provides enjoyable, satisfying work for you and others. As Robert Louis Stevenson put it, 'My idea of man's chief end was to enrich the world with things of beauty and have a fairly good time myself while doing so.'

That is a noble aspiration indeed. I have written this book to help those of you who share it.

1. How Do You Want to Live?

Too much capitalism does not mean too many capitalists,
but too few capitalists.
— G. K. Chesterton

Periodically, I go to visit my tycoon friend John Brown for business advice. John made his millions from publishing magazines, the best known of which is the adult comic *Viz*. As the cricket plays on a huge screen and assistants bring us glasses of water, he sits behind his spotless, minimalist desk in an office on the Portobello Road, boasting about his successes, and then he abuses me. 'The *Idler* is not a business!' he shouts. 'It's a lifestyle!'

What does he mean? Well, in tycoon circles, to write off your project as a 'lifestyle business' is a terrible insult. People who choose, for example, to move to the countryside and work there, and not to slave away sixteen hours a day in a City skyscraper in the pursuit of riches, are snootily dismissed by the twice-divorced and usually very boring money-getters as 'lifestylers'. The tycoons consider any business that does not make a ton of cash as nothing more than a hobby.

The tycoons are not interested in one bookshop or one café. They are interested in nine hundred bookshops or cafés. They want scale. They want to turn a thousand pounds into a million as quickly as possible. They have no passion for any particular product. They have a passion for making money. They love business. And their business could be dog food, oil, insurance or spare-bedroom rental: they don't really care.

But we bohemians, we're different. We want to enjoy our work *and* enjoy our everyday life *and* make a living from it, all at once. We want to be creative. We value freedom over money. We're those naive souls who want to turn our 'passion project', as the rather nauseating phrase goes, into a business.

But what sort of business will this be? Self-employed plumber or Richard Branson? Victoria and I are often asked, 'Is this something you are doing just for fun, or do you want to build it up into something you can sell?' In other words, is this just a hobby, or are you ambitious for it?

So the first thing to ask yourself when going into business is: what is the point of all this? Do you crave vast wealth – or freedom? Do you want to communicate a message? Do you want to have three-day weekends? Do you want to have fun? Do you want to help people? Do you want the satisfaction that comes from creating something of beauty, or of utility? Do you want a lie-in? Pop stars often say that their motivation for starting a band was that they wanted to find a way of earning a living that didn't involve getting up at eight o'clock every morning.

What is Your Idea of the Good Life?

The ancient Greeks had a concept called *eudaimonia*. It meant happiness, in the sense of fulfilment. And, in a literal sense, it meant being at one with your daemon, or inner spirit. Happy people are those who have found their purpose, or what was called their 'natural genius' in the eighteenth century. You need to think about what your 'good life' would consist of.

Many people are content with running a lifestyle business, with being a sole operator. They are the small shopkeepers, the consultants, the taxi drivers, the builders, the plumbers, the painters and decorators. What these lifestylers have in common is that they enjoy their work – more or less – and earn a sufficient income to make ends meet. And, for many of us bohemian types, that is all we need to attain our own particular version of the good life.

The café round the corner from our office is an example of a lifestyle business. It's run by Alfredo and his son. They don't make millions, but they enjoy serving customers and they get by. To run your own small business of this sort is, I think, quite a noble aspiration. It is a rich life and never boring.

Lifestylers come in many shapes and sizes. I have a friend who makes a decent living as an independent tailor. He has no overheads, no office and no ambition to launch an international fashion label. He enjoys making the odd suit. His costs are very low and he enjoys total freedom.

Then there are my friends Gavin Turk and Deborah

Curtis. Gavin is a successful Brit artist, and the couple also run a brilliant children's education charity called the House of Fairy Tales. We often find ourselves in charge of adjacent 'stalls' at summer festivals. From simple beginnings, Deborah has built a sizeable organization which brings joy to thousands every year. I don't think they have made a fortune, but they can live.

Finally, I should mention the example of another former journalist, Jean-Paul Flintoff. In addition to doing fun stuff like writing novels about Queen Anne, he has retrained as a life coach. He charges a very high hourly rate and has a handful of customers. This means he can do work he enjoys *and* he has time left over to pursue more speculative projects. For Jean-Paul, being a sole trader means freedom. He has no ambitions to take on any staff.

Now, the danger is that by doing something noble and interesting and not just contenting yourself with selling crude oil or dog food or pizza – as the real titans do – you could be condemning yourself to years of sweat and toil for scant reward. If your work is, nonetheless, fulfilling, this may not put you off – in which case, you have achieved *eudaimonia*. And that's no small achievement: Aristotle thought of *eudaimonia* as the highest possible human good. Not a bad end for a self-employed plumber.

It could be, though, that attaining your version of the good life requires a little more than running a lifestyle business. This doesn't mean you have to be a money-obsessed tycoon; bohemians are the driving forces behind plenty of what John Brown would refer to as 'real' businesses.

For instance, a very different example of a successful

bohemian in business is my old friend Dan Kieran, a successful author who worked at the *Idler* for a while. When the bottom fell out of the publishing business, he found, simply put, that he needed a job. But instead of applying for one, he and some friends developed a new crowdfunding publishing idea, Unbound, and went around raising investment. Dan had a simple pitch: 'When I was a writer, hundreds of thousands of people bought my books,' he says. 'I realized that I didn't have the name and address of a single one of them.'

With Unbound, he would build up a database of people who were prepared to spend real money on supporting books. Dan has ambitions far beyond lifestyle for his business. 'I want this to be massive,' he says.

Dan turned out to be a brilliant salesman. He raised two million pounds from angel investors and his company now employs over fifteen staff. He has become a CEO. He takes a reasonable salary, goes to work every day and is building something which will potentially not only have value but also produce a lot of beautiful books and provide authors and his staff with a living – which is a great achievement. When I asked him whether he found it stressful being beholden to his investors, he said that it was simply part of his job. 'They are funding me, and I have a responsibility towards them.'

Then there is a sort of halfway house between the two types of business, such as that operated by Nigel House from Rough Trade record shops. He does what he loves, which is to introduce his customers to great new music. He opened the first branch in 1976, and there are now four: two in London, one in Nottingham and one in

Brooklyn, USA. This is still a small business, but it's real, it's growing; Nigel employs thirty staff. Recently, he has attracted investment. He told me that an investor said to him, 'Rough Trade is not a business; it's a passion.' It's not a business in the way that selling office furniture is a business – but Nigel still has to be businesslike about it.

You couldn't say that Nigel has made a fortune from what he does. That may come in the future, though, in his words, 'My wife says to me it's always "jam tomorrow" with you.' But he just adores music and his everyday life. He loves being behind the counter selling records, making recommendations. His life has purpose and meaning, and this has been more important to him than making piles of cash. And so he is still there, pulling up the shutters just off the Portobello Road in the morning, with a pencil behind his ear and in a Thrasher T-shirt.

It is this that all the above have in common. They are doing what they want to do. They have taken responsibility. They are not slaves. The freedom is more important than the money. These entrepreneurs have taken control of their lives and worked out – often after many years of trial and error – a system that suits them.

How Well Do You Know Yourself?

Now, you may not have the right personality to be a CEO. After all, it's not a great job. You sit there while people hurl problems at you all day.

Acceptance of that fact is not an admission of failure.

6

In fact, it is the key to deciding what the good life entails for you. You must find out who you are and proceed on the basis of that knowledge. Everyone in business will tell you again and again that there is no point struggling to do things which are against your nature. If you decide to grow your business, as time passes, you will find professionals to do the things you're not so good at.

'Isn't it obvious,' said Socrates (according to his friend Xenophon), 'that people are successful, when they know themselves, and failures, when they do not? Those who know themselves know what suits them best, because they can distinguish between what they can and what they cannot do. By doing what they know about, they meet their own needs and achieve their ends; while by steering clear of things they don't understand, they avoid failure and mistakes.'

When it comes to the *Idler*, I now have ambitions beyond a lifestyle business. I'd like to communicate these ideas around the world. I want to grow. I want to build a trusted provider of quirky British educational resources and entertainment. I want to sell more subscriptions to the magazine. What I want to create is a business that improves people's lives and which makes a profit. The real pleasure for me of doing *Idler* business is the impact on the lives of our readers, customers and fans. They love the fact that we exist. We help them to find happiness. And that is the whole point.

In terms of my everyday life, I just want to carry on working. My ideal day would go as follows: I like to work on my own in the morning, doing creative stuff – writing, editing, dreaming up new products. That can be done in the library, at home or in a café. And in the afternoon, I like to hang around in my office and work with my team. In the evening I want to go home at seven, drink beer, chat to my family and read books. And I want to be not in debt and not to worry about money.

That's pretty much it. I'm not bothered about cars, skiing holidays, big houses, clothes or any of those baubles. I am happy when I am making things. If I make proper money, I will spend it on taking people to restaurants and on what are now called 'experiences', not on stuff.

Bohemians and idlers often, paradoxically, have this in common: their work is the most important thing in their life. This was true for Picasso, and it is true for Richard Branson. It is true for me. I will never retire. I will continue reading and writing till the day I die.

The key difference between the lifestyle business and the 'real' business is accountability. If you grow beyond a lifestyle business, then you are accountable to other people. You have to pay wages and you have to report back to your fellow directors and to your shareholders. You cannot suddenly decide to go and live on a Scottish island for six months. There is a thing called governance, which means the process of getting things done. It means that you create a board of directors. You have meetings. You apportion tasks. You are held to account.

This sort of accountability, and the feeling of selling oneself that may seem to go along with it, does not suit all bohemians. I recently went to interview singer-songwriter Cerys Matthews, who had huge success in nineties band Catatonia. After a few years, she told me, she had to get out of the music business, because she no longer felt free:

Cerys: The kickback of the success is that it becomes a business, a commercial enterprise, and there're responsibilities involved. There are people getting wages because of the success you had.

TH: So you went in for creative freedom and not having a job or a boss, and then you found you were trapped.

Cerys: You are a cog in the system.

This is possibly what drove Amy Winehouse and Kurt Cobain to early graves. They could not handle being cogs. They could not handle monetizing their content. That was not the reason they become bohemian singers. The strolling player may not be temperamentally adapted to being in business. Other bands – let's say, Coldplay and U2 – are very happy being CEOs. Damien Hirst is another example of a happy artist/CEO: he loves the responsibility of employing loads of staff.

So, if you don't want to be a CEO, if you don't want all that responsibility, then you may decide to stay small.

Or take one step at a time: first, it's just you; then, you find a partner; then a staff member . . . and so on.

Nothing Wrong with Growth

If, like me, as a good bohemian, you have a soft spot for the gentle, ethical economics promoted by people like E. F. Schumacher, author of *Small is Beautiful*, then you might have heard the idea that growth is a bad thing. The argument goes roughly like this: the pursuit of growth for its own sake is wrong. It is based on false logic, because you cannot keep growing for ever. Companies that are publicly shared are forced to grow because their share-holders want the shares to increase in value. Otherwise, they wouldn't bother buying them. And that turns the company into a ravenous monster which puts share price above customers, quality, ethics and beauty. The ethical economists set themselves up as enemies of the Chicago school of economists: Milton Friedman and the rest of them.

Obviously, there is a lot of truth in the argument that there are natural limits to growth. The problem is that you are made to feel guilty if you admit that you, too, would like a business that grows. You feel that an eco-warrior like George Monbiot is going to wag his finger at you and accuse you of wasting natural resources.

But growth is natural. After all, a seed grows into a seedling, the seedling sprouts and produces seeds for regeneration, the seeds are dispersed and the plant dies. Animals and humans grow. Your business, if you choose to create one that is more than just a lifestyle, can be seen as a growing and ever-changing plant that you are tending, watering and cultivating. In fact, 'cultivation' may be a better word than 'growth' for the process we're talking about: the cultivation of a small business.

Growth is good. Of course I want to 'increase my estate', as they said in the old days. I think the more important issue may well be the pace. Investors look for a rapid rate of growth: they are excited by a steep upward curve. They call it 'hockey stick' growth. I think that is actually very rare, and what we are looking for is some sort of 'slow business' idea. We need to create a business philosophy that is sensible in that you make a profit, but which does not drive you to distraction with silly pressures. A small step each day. People in business are always trying to hurry you for a decision. Take your time. Sleep on it.

Write It Down

My advice now is to go for a long walk and think about your life. Then come home, sit down with a notebook and write down what you want to do and how you want to live. What brings you pleasure, and what brings you satisfaction? What would your ideal day look like? That is the first step. Once you have done that, read the second chapter, which introduces you to the fundamental concepts of good business.

2. All about the Money

Rich bohemians have more fun than poor bohemians.
  – Charles Handy, interviewed for the *Idler*

Bohemians affect disdain for Mammon. They live for art and life, so they say. But if you don't address financial issues in a grown-up fashion, you'll end up poor, which is no fun at all. You'll be paying absurd fines and interest charges to the bankers, bailiffs and tax-collectors. They might not burn down your straw hut, but they will knock on your door. It has happened to us. Your chaos will do nothing but profit your oppressor.

So, you need to get comfortable, before you start, with the idea of making money. Respect may be nice but, as punk poet John Cooper Clarke once wisely said to me, 'Respect don't pay the rent.' Making a profit is good. It means that you are creating a sustainable business that can last for many years, employ people and spread joy.

If you don't make money from your business, you'll either be bailing out the business from other funds or you'll go bankrupt. And either outcome will be preceded by a lorry-load of stress. I keep hearing that 50 per cent of new businesses fail within the first five years. It's like the Grand National: steep odds.

The first point is that you will need some money, most probably, to start your business. If you are planning to work as a consultant with no overheads, or a freelance journalist, then the money required for entry is pretty minimal: enough to buy a computer, perhaps. When I set up an ad agency with my friend Gav, we had no set-up costs at all beyond a bit of equipment. And in the first year we had no office costs because we squatted in the corner of someone else's office in return for helping them out a bit. When you start a business, it's sensible to keep your overheads down to an absolute minimum. That means being very thrifty and very frugal: work from home or from cafés; don't buy clothes; and make a packed lunch.

The great management guru Charles Handy says that, as far as money goes, you have to look after yourself. He reckons you may need to do something else as well as your 'passion project' to earn money, particularly in the early stages of a new business. He writes that life can be divided into your passion, your duty and money:

> Passion, duty, and money are three aspects, part of a continuing portfolio. And things change over time. So at one time money is dominant, followed by your duty, and then your passion. And your passion has to be pushed to the back because your children are growing up and you need money. Over time, you can change that around. But you always have to have those three components.

My mistake has often been to prioritize the passion at the expense of duty and money. I have always done what

I wanted to do work-wise and have never prostituted myself. That is not actually such a good idea, as it can lead to frugal living beyond the point of comfort. 'Why can't we have cereals, like other families?' my children would ask. And they have always found our old bangers really embarrassing.

That is why I am encouraging all bohemian business-people to think carefully about money. You want to avoid a situation where you are constantly chasing your tail financially. And that may mean finding a reasonable amount of investment in your idea. After all, if you have no money, you will find the going very tough indeed. As Dr Johnson wrote:

> The mournful truth is everywhere confessed,
> Slow rises worth by poverty oppressed.

Memberships and Subscriptions

You could consider some sort of subscription-service business model. I am told that subscription and member-ship services are, like, so hot right now. People love being members of a cool club and getting stuff in the post. There is even a new book on the subject called *The Membership Economy: Find Your Super Users, Master the Forever Transaction, and Build Recurring Revenue*. That is a very beautiful and almost poetic title, I think. It reaches a pitch of existential intensity. The book reckons that subscription-model businesses are the way to go. I certainly think that they would suit the bohemian who is looking at providing high-quality services for relatively small numbers of people and not looking to compete with Amazon or Asos.

Companies like Graze (love their faux-hippy marketing with those irritating little arrows everywhere – not), Riverford Organic (a brilliant food-box-delivery scheme) and Patreon (a kind of crowd-patron scheme for artists and musicians) are getting their customers to sign up and to make regular payments. If you offer this kind of service, you need to ensure that you can supply what you say you can. It is all too easy to get carried away with promising fantastic rewards to your potential supporters, only to find that fulfilling these pledges can be onerous. Think ahead: are you going to regret offering every one of your supporters a self-penned poem singing their praises? Are you really going to send them a leather-bound copy of your book?

For our own part, in 2016, we relaunched the *Idler* as a quarterly print journal. In the three months leading up to the release of the first issue, I sold around six hundred subscriptions to people on our mailing list. In this way we managed to raise £20,000 before we'd even printed issue one.

We also sell annual memberships. This is a scheme whereby our members get access to special areas of our website and discounts on the books and online courses we sell.

The ideal for a small business would be to sign up your customers on a direct-debit scheme. The problem is that no bank will offer the incipient small business a direct-debit service. I know: I have been turned down countless times. They tell you that the risk is too great, and that the bank will offer you direct debit only if you give them a huge pile of cash as an insurance policy. So you're in a Catch-22 situation.

But there are ways around this. You could use a service like Shopify which will allow you to take recurring payments. Or you could contact Gocardless, who will arrange it for you. My advice is not to bother calling your bank direct, as they will just laugh at you.

You could also use PayPal's subscription-payment system to get the cash in. PayPal charges quite a hefty commission – 3.5 per cent of each sale, compared to around 1.9 per cent taken by most credit- and debit-card companies – but they transfer the money to you instantly. We used PayPal exclusively for our first three years of trading, and it was a great way to get the ball rolling before we could afford to look into alternative options.

Jumping on the subscription bandwagon isn't for everyone, though. Maybe subscriptions don't suit what you do. Let's look at some other sources of cash.

Money from the Bank

When we launched the *Idler* magazine in 1993, I raised £800 from family and friends. I sold six-month, twelve-month and lifetime subscriptions. A couple of well-to-do friends put in one hundred quid. That gave us enough to print a thousand copies of the first issue. We had a magazine.

This was a good starting point, and it might work for you, too, but it inevitably comes with a downside. Family and friends can be tricky investors because they want to advise you, and they may change their mind about wanting to help you (more on that in Chapter 13). Banks, on the other hand, just collect the interest and leave you alone.

Charles Handy reckons that, whatever your bohemian ideals, the bank is your best source of finance. I managed to get a loan from the bank. I had opened an account some years previously to run the *Idler* magazine, which at that time was a very small business, turning over £25,000 a year. Luckily, I had run that account well and the bank lent us £13,000, to be paid back over five years.

This loan came at a price: we paid about five grand in interest. In the same period, we earned zero per cent on a nine-grand deposit we had paid on day one. Clearly, we should have become bankers, not booksellers.

Money from Remortgaging

To get our real-life Idler Academy bookshop moving, we needed to hire staff, rent a shop and buy stock, as well as pay lawyers and cover a hundred other trifling and infuriating expenses. I called my old friend Bill Drummond for some wise counsel. He is perhaps not the best person to ask for financial advice, since he famously burned a million pounds. But he has had a great career doing exactly what he wants – in 1991, his band the KLF became the biggest-selling singles act in the world – and I respect him hugely.

'I always remortgaged when it came to business,' said Bill. 'I know everyone says, "Don't put your house on the line," but to me this was the best way of raising money, since I took full responsibility. I funded the KLF this way and was able to keep the profits.'

Remortgaging is not available to young people without a house, of course. But we had a three-bedroom house in Shepherds Bush and managed to borrow £40,000 against it. This itself was stressful. We had a very high loan-to-value ratio, but a low income, both Victoria and I being self-employed entrepreneurs. Banks, like governments, pretend to like the self-employed. But, actually, they hate us. It appears that banks would rather you had any old crap job, as long as it is full time and for a big company, rather than be a freelancer.

There were many moments during the mortgage application process when I felt like giving up. Our first application was refused, so we applied again. The wheels ground slowly and, meanwhile, we had taken a risk by signing a lease on a shop and engaging the services of a shop-fitter. I remember visiting the shop and seeing Polish painters with ladders in it, merrily working away. I had no idea how we were going to pay them if the second application fell through. I recall driving through the Devon countryside where we lived, staring into space in a paralysis of panic, with Victoria by my side doing the same thing, our three children in the back.

I remember Robin Birley, the owner of swanky Mayfair night-club 5 Hertford Street, saying to Nicky Dunne, the proprietor of fabled Mayfair bookshop Heywood Hill: 'It must be nice running a little bookshop, Nicky. No stress.' No, no, no! It is one of the most difficult things you can do these days, in the age of Amazon. Beware! I have just had an email from the owners of another small magazine which ran a bookshop, a great company called Slightly Foxed. They, like us, closed their shop when the rent went up. They wrote, 'We found having a retail outlet the most stressful part of the business, what with rent, rates, etc. It's a lovely idea, having a bookshop, but quite difficult in reality.'

For us, there was no possibility of raising much money from friends or family. My father has no money. Victoria's parents were, very sensibly, somewhat sceptical about our idea of a small bookshop and café teaching Latin, and sent us letters urging us not to do it. So, a remortgage, I think, was a good option.

Should You Seek Investment?

Victoria and I, then, took on most of the financial risk ourselves when setting up the Idler Academy. We did approach a couple of investors at an early stage, but they said no. And who could blame them? An independent bookshop in an obscure corner of Bayswater did not exactly seem like a hot money-making opportunity. 'I see, mid-life-crisis centre,' said John Brown when I showed him the shop. 'Marginal at best.' We would have to pursue this dream alone, at least to begin with.

Four years on, we attracted our first serious investor. At the time of writing, we employ three members of staff. And now we are busy moving on to the next stage by raising money from angel investors and from our readers and fans. We have turned a hobby into a small business. Now we want to grow to medium size, by which I mean a business which is turning over annually £400,000 or more.

For me, going after investment was a good idea, as it suits the expansionist frame of mind I increasingly find myself in. For the ten years up to now, I ran the *Idler* pretty much as a hobby. That suited me at the time, because I was writing books and Victoria and I had young children.

But investment brings responsibility. The investors want a business which, in their words, will 'scale'. That means: 'has enormous potential for growth'. What investors want is to put in a million pounds now and withdraw a billion pounds in ten years' time. They're looking to get massive returns. Most of their investments, they say, tend to fail. Therefore, paydays from businesses which succeed in 'scaling' are what they live for. In order to secure this payback, though, investors might force you to make tough decisions, or even make them for you. The founder of Office shoes, Richard Wharton, complains that investors sacked all his friends, the ones he'd started the business with.

To get to the point of payback, you might have to dwell in purgatory, or even hell, for ten, fifteen or twenty years. Do you really want to do that? Do you have the right personality for it? Would you find it fun? Or are you a creative, sensitive person who would hate to be a ruthless CEO?

Investors can be a pain. Even small investors can turn out to be more trouble than they're worth. You'll get a load of unsolicited advice from someone who doesn't necessarily know what they're talking about. You'll also essentially be indebted to them; and one of our purposes here is to escape indebtedness, because being debt-free, rather than actually having money, leads to happiness.

However, having surveyed the business landscape, it is pretty obvious that businesses that grow quickly attract investment. So we're now launching an equity round to fund our next stage.

How to Crowdfund

As I write, I am preparing a load of documents for our forthcoming sale of shares via Crowdcube. Yes, we are crowdfunding. This internet platform, which launched in 2010, has been attracting a lot of headlines. The idea is that a large number of investors buy shares in your company and you use the money to accelerate its growth.

As we have a goodly number of readers and fans – what you would call a 'crowd' – I thought that this would be the ideal way to raise money. But I would like to warn anyone who is considering raising money through crowdfunding that preparing your company for a share sale of this sort requires more work than you could ever conceive. You will have to prepare detailed spreadsheets outlining your projected earnings and outgoings over five years, and you will have to explain every assumption you have made along the way. You will have to learn about balance sheets and cash flow. You will have to write and rewrite a business plan (more on that later). You will have to script and film a video clip. You will have to deal with the slow-moving wheels of government bureaucracy.

You will also be asked to raise 40 per cent of the money you need to come up with before the official campaign begins. That means writing to your fans and taking your proposal round to various investors. You will end up feeling like a *Dragon's Den* contestant. So, before you throw yourself into a crowdfunding campaign, whatever you do, don't assume it's the easy option to secure investment.

As I mentioned, the workload is immense. I had a coffee with a venture capitalist who has worked for thirty years at the cutting edge of finance with some of the biggest companies in the world in order to tell him about the *Idler*. I explained what I'd had to do for Crowdcube, and he was amazed. 'That is an absurd amount of work for a small company and a small amount of money,' he said. I have since heard that a crowdfunding application of this kind typically takes two to three people six months of practically full-time work.

Another downside can be that you tend to take your eye off the everyday running of your business. Sales, in our case, have certainly suffered while I have had my head immersed in spreadsheets.

However, I do not regret the work I put in for one moment, because it has helped me to clarify exactly what is going on within the *Idler* and what we want to do with it. Even if we fail to raise the money, the rigorous process I've been through has undoubtedly increased the value of the company, because it has made us more efficient and focused. I am also anticipating good PR from the campaign: regardless of the outcome, it has been an invaluable opportunity to reach potential customers.

My advice if you are considering a share sale via crowd-funding is to take your time. Give it six months. If possible, talk to someone who has successfully raised money in this way. And while you're piling resources into trying to get your business off the ground, don't forget to reserve some energy for keeping yourself above the breadline.

What Will You Live On?

On an every-day level, you are going to need cash to live on. It may not be possible for the business to pay you anything in the early years. Luke Johnson, the serial entrepreneur whose investments include Pizza Express and Patisserie Valerie, and who has been chairman of Channel 4 and the Royal Society of Arts, says that taking money out of a new business is a mistake made by amateurs. Any excess cash should go straight back into paying bills, making new products, buying new machines, employing more people.

Prepare yourself for grinding poverty. Reduce all your outgoings to a minimum. That means no holidays, no taxis, no meals out, no expensive car, no shopping trips. These things mean precisely nothing to me, so it's not a huge hardship for me to live frugally. As long as I have beer and books and I am not in debt, then I am happy. It pays at this stage to be Epicurean in the true sense, which is to live well on little.

You need to ask yourself: how am I going to live while

this business gets going? Can I pay myself a small salary, or would the money be better spent on marketing or creating a new product or taking on more staff? In our case, I reckoned, eventually, that it would be best to delegate as much as possible to members of staff and leave myself free to earn money and develop new ideas. The trick when employing staff is to find people who are better than you at doing one particular thing. We'll return to that in Chapter 12.

This approach, however, meant that, in the early years, we took virtually nothing out of the business to pay ourselves. Often, it was the other way round: the VAT bill would come in, and I had to pay it from my personal bank account.

You may well need to keep the day job at the outset, or at least a part-time job. Remember Charles Handy's advice about passion, duty and money and try to keep all three in balance. In the first year of the Idler Academy, I was writing both a newspaper and a magazine column. So at least we knew we could eat. I would also get the occasional cheque for €800 for selling a book to Estonia. John Brown advised me not to 'turn down paid work for the *Idler*'. So think ahead about income because, ideally, you will *not* be taking money out of the business for the first three years or so. As Luke Johnson says, that is an amateur's mistake.

Having said that, it was handy having a shop. There was always twenty quid in the till that I could take out for emergencies (as long as it was properly accounted for as 'return of loan', of course).

Dealing with Debt

As should be clear by now, if you want to create your own business, you have to accept that you are entering a world of money. This is not a vanity project. And you may well run up debts. Well, some entrepreneurs love debt. It turns them on. The bigger the debt, the better. They don't care. I have friends who borrow silly amounts for their silly mortgages, and it doesn't seem to bother them. 'Money is cheap right now,' they say. Unfortunately, I am not one of those people. Debt worries me.

And debt really worries Victoria. At certain points, she has run up small debts on her credit card to bail out the business. And every day she has woken up in the morning, sighed, and said, 'I feel sick.' Being in debt made her feel physically ill. And I don't like it either; it's when my account goes into the black that I start feeling happy. When it is in the red, I start feeling stressed out. Maybe it's crazy to let an abstract concept like money bother me that much. If I have enough to eat, then what is the problem?

But either through social conditioning, or from nature, this is what I feel.

I wonder whether people running big businesses feel this. I reckon they don't worry about it. They will borrow millions, lose millions, make millions, and start again. They have the hide of a rhinoceros. It would be interesting, perhaps, to study their mental habits, which could be said to be close to the attitudes of mind encouraged by

Eastern religions. They say: the world is a fiction, it is created by our thoughts, so nothing really matters. Develop a carefree attitude. Live in the moment. Release the ego.

Ideally, you would do both. You would remain detached while also embracing an ethic of service. Your business should help people. You should improve their lives. That can be very satisfying. I really enjoy selling books and courses. There is nothing better than to receive a letter saying, 'The Idler Academy Book Club [from which we send out a book of our choice each month] is the best present I've ever had,' or to hear a customer say, 'I no longer need therapy now that I take ukulele lessons at the Idler Academy.'

Above all, don't lose track of why you're doing this.

Enjoy It

You must enjoy your business and your work; otherwise, there really is no point. You may well find that the very thing which you hoped would bring you money and freedom instead brings in little money and a lot of headaches. Therefore, the everyday must, in the main, be a source of satisfaction, and even pleasure and fun. And you must somehow enjoy the lows as well as the highs. You must enjoy dealing with problems day in, day out.

I would recommend doing a 'fun audit' every few months, just to make sure that you're not becoming depressed. If things are going wrong, change your system. For example, I was trying to work at home with

Victoria, but she drove me crazy, wandering in and asking about passwords, or laundry, or payments for the children's school trips. So I decided to walk out of the house every morning at ten to nine and spend the hours from nine till one in the local library, where I could really concentrate, free of distraction.

Recently, more often than not, I've been working on the dreaded business plan. More than any other business tool, this is the one most guaranteed to instil fear deep into the heart of the bohemian in business. But fear no more; read on.

3. How to Write a Business Plan

*I'm afraid those two words together still petrify me with
their dullness. They are whatever the opposite of buzzwords
is – sigh words?*
– Murphy Williams, marshmallow entrepreneur

Business plans are practically impossible. They are like
pinning down a live butterfly. How can you fix an idea
when the world is in flux? And how do you know what
will happen in the future? Sadly, though, business plans
are an absolute must.

Many moons ago, when I decided to start a magazine,
I went on a council-run course for unemployed – or
unemployable – people wanting to start their own business. The pupils were mostly lazybones like me who
couldn't stand the idea of a proper job. Alongside some
basic instruction about fixed costs and variable costs (of
which more later), the importance of writing a business
plan was impressed on us. We needed to make a stab at
guessing our turnover and profits, and we needed to
explain what it was we planned to do.

I remember at the time that we little wannabe
business-builders scorned the idea. How could we

possibly know what was going to happen in our business? Were we soothsayers?

Also, it wasn't as if anyone was going to invest in our project. After all, we were all on the dole. So what was the point? Why couldn't we just go with the flow? Don't hold me down to your plans, man. I am free! I scorn your prison bars!

Reader, I never wrote a business plan back then. I just produced issue one of the *Idler* and sort of hoped it would sell. It worked out all right – the title went on to be co-published by the *Guardian* and the magazine is still going – but today I still wish I had followed the advice I was given and written some kind of plan. Partly because it forces you to think through your idea very carefully indeed. It is a statement as well as a plan.

There are certain business advisors out there who tell you to reject what they call 'bullshit business plans'. Their point is that you cannot see into the future. But this is not the right attitude. You must, I'm afraid, write some sort of business plan, just in the same way that, when I was planning this book, I first wrote a list of chapters with their titles and a short precis of each. A business plan is a campaign, a strategy, an outline of what you want to do and how you plan to do it. And you need to write one whether or not you are looking for finance. 'Writing a business plan is essential for yourself, not just for backers,' advises John Brown.

When we started the Idler Academy, I sat down to write one of these fiendish documents. And I found the process of writing it to be of enormous help. The discipline of following a structure and thinking through every out-going and source of revenue clarified my thoughts.

I did not write our first business plan with the aim of securing funding. We already had a bank loan, had remortgaged and raised a few grand from friends to get us going. I wrote it to pin it down for myself. Writing a business plan is like tidying your brain. It's the process of gathering your thoughts and dreams into one place.

What, exactly, though, is a business plan? Briefly put, it is a proposal, it is a dream, it is a description of what you want to do and how you are going to do it, and who you are going to do it with. Luke Johnson says that a business plan should be fun and chatty and avoid business bullshit. It should look at what is going to happen over the next twelve to eighteen months and not beyond. It is a document that you might want to show to a bank in order to request a loan. Or you can use it to raise money from investors.

The strange thing about a business plan is that it attempts to be a crystal ball. It predicts the future, and everyone knows that predicting the future is impossible. It's like gambling: how can you possibly foretell the out-come of sporting events? You can't. It's a guess.

The good thing is that everybody understands that business plans are fantasy. And dreams can come true. I know this from my own experience: I had the vision of a magazine, a book, an absinthe-importing business and a bookshop, and they have all come into being.

Your business plan should tell a compelling story. It should present a problem that you are going to fix. For ex-ample, everyone feels that they don't know enough about

Greek philosophy. So we are going to teach them. Or people are stressed out. We are going to help them to calm down.

In the case of the Idler Academy, there is a clear story. Put briefly, Victoria and I put on a series of highbrow talks at a festival and sold coffees, teas and beautiful books. We enjoyed it so much that we set up a similar project two years later in a large marquee at a literary festival in Cornwall, and attached a café to the tent. Again, we enjoyed it so much that we remortgaged our house, took out a five-year lease on a shop in Notting Hill and ran an Academy full time.

Your business plan should first and foremost be a document for you. It should help you to get a clear grip on your idea and how you are going to make it happen.

When thinking about your business plan, you could do a lot worse than to sign on to a crowdfunding company as an investor. Study the pitches on the site and read their business plans. Most of them are really boring, so add some humour and wit, because investors are humans, too.

My advice would be to start by jotting down a few notes on each section (see below). And keep it short.

The Idea

Go for a long walk. Then spend a page writing down what your business does. Tell the story so far and describe the mix of products and services you offer. Try a stream-of-consciousness approach. Imagine you are telling someone you have just met what it is that you do. Don't worry if it is gobbledegook.

Then, try to sum up your business in a few words. Simplify and clarify. This is much, much harder than it sounds. When it comes to writing, cutting is harder than adding. But what you are aiming for is what business-people call the 'elevator pitch'. An example might be 'dry-stone walling training for the over-fifties' or 'high school for grown-ups' or 'healthy fruit drinks with nothing added'.

The conventional advice here, given in all business books, is that you have identified a problem in society and that you intend to solve this problem with the product or service you are proposing to sell. In the case of the *Idler*, we felt that people were (and are) feeling stressed out and under-educated. So the intention was to bring some fun and fulfilment into people's lives through singing and dancing lessons and other events, and also to fill the gaps in their knowledge with books, talks and online courses. We broke all the rules by inventing a Latin motto that no one understands: *libertas per cultum* – freedom through education.

These days, you are also supposed to think about what is called your 'mission'. And your 'passion'. These are the slightly odd quasi-religious terms that are used in business these days. You will need to dream up some sort of mission statement, for example: our mission is to become the world's leading retailer of dog-cushion covers.

Try to nail down your proposition in a succinct fifty words. Even if you are a one-man band, like Jean-Paul Flintoff, former journalist and current life coach, this is a useful exercise. His website puts it simply: 'I'm a speaker. I write books. I'm a journalist. I'm a coach. I'm a maker.'

For what it's worth, here is my latest attempt at a fifty-word pitch:

> The *Idler* is a much-loved publishing and events brand with a mission to help people find fulfilment and freedom in everyday life. Early testing of paid-for online courses in philosophy, ukulele, etc. has proved successful, and we plan to roll out an ambitious on-demand learning programme in the arts, creative entrepreneurship and practical skills.

The Market

In this section you need to describe the people your products and services are aimed at. Think it through. Who are they? How are you going to improve their lives? How will you meet them? What are they lacking that you will provide? Do you have any evidence or testimonials from any research into the market that you have already done? Can you provide some figures that will show how this group of people is growing?

In the case of the *Idler*, we want to reach self-employed people and people who want to be self-employed. We want to reach brainy, dissatisfied people who read books, listen to Radio 4 and like learning.

Where are they? What newspapers do they read? What

books would they buy? Where do they live? What do they want out of life? How do they use social media?

Whether you are a permaculture teacher or a pianist, you need to think about who might hire you and make a list of these people so that you can approach them.

The Team

Who will be doing all this?

You may have decided that you want to be a sole operator, that you will be a one-man band, in which case this part of the business plan is fairly easily written. My friend the filmmaker Dave Hunt, who films our courses, does everything in his business himself: 'I like the flexibility. I can take my children to work in the morning and then work an extra two hours. I can always hire in extra people to do bigger jobs. The technology allows me to work from home. The downside is that you can spend too much time on your own.'

But even if you're a sole trader like Dave, you need to think about your team. You will need some help: Who will do your accounts? Who will be your advisors? Who will you employ to help out at busy times? Who will be your sounding board? Should you find a business partner?

You also need someone on the team who has experience in the sector you are going into. That may, of course, be you. When we started the Idler Academy, Victoria and I were the only members of the team. We both have years of experience in event organizing, writing, communication and journalism. But we had none at all in bookselling, running a café, managing staff or indeed in running a proper business. We would have done better to find a bookseller and an experienced numbers person right at the beginning. In fact, we did attempt to employ a very experienced bookshop manager, but he dropped out at the last minute, leaving the two of us with one junior staff member who had no experience. He did his best but, in the end, the strain was too much and he left after about a year. We gave him far too much to do and put far too much responsibility on his shoulders. No wonder he quit with a bad feeling about us. Later, Julian, an experienced bookseller, joined us, and things started to improve.

In your business plan, you'll need to present a short, accurate biography, of perhaps three hundred words, about each member of your team. Don't overuse clichés like 'passionate' and 'committed'. Concentrate on the facts of what this person has actually done in the past, not what they want to do. Track record is important. You, and your potential investors, will want to know that your team can make things happen. Put yourself into the mindset of a potential investor: would you remortgage your house and put £50,000 into this idea? Would you put £10,000 into this idea? An investor is going to want a return of considerably more than the 5 per cent per annum they might get from the bank. They are also going to want to have fun and do something interesting. So think about how you can enhance the every-day life of a potential investor, beyond just making money for them.

Your Wise Men

You should also assemble an advisory board, not only to help with your business plan but for guidance further down the line, too. These are people, possibly friends, who work in similar areas to you and have been successful in business. Study them, talk to them, find out how they work and think, and ask their advice.

Find people who will be happy to tell you that you are being an idiot. After all, you are not in business to make yourself feel good. You do not want flatterers. Our advisors include John Brown, and Dan Kieran, former *Idler* employee and now CEO of Unbound. We have recently welcomed James Pembroke, publisher of the *Oldie* magazine, as our unofficial chairman. He is helping with budgets and accounts. Mentors are hugely important. They can give you good contacts and a healthy dose of reality. In essence, they bring clarity.

The problem I have with wise men is that I tend to go along with the most recent person I have spoken to. 'John says we should stop selling tea towels!' 'Dan says we should go digital!' To prevent this kind of knee-jerk reaction, discipline yourself to take the advice of your wise men and then let it gestate in your mind. Seek out further advice and gradually, slowly, work out what you should do.

The Competition

Include some material in your business plan about your competition. Become obsessed by your competition. You may think you have none, but you do. The Idler Academy may look like a new idea but, really, we're competing with existing providers of evening courses and educational resources. Such classes have been around for ever and are very well run by others. What will they do when you start selling in competition with them? And do other, similar businesses actually make a profit? Reading their tweets and looking at their website will not give an accurate picture of what is really going on in their business.

One guide is Facebook. Take a look at the Facebook pages of businesses like yours. Line them up on the 'insights' section. And if you have the time and a bit of cash, you can look them up on the Companies House website to see how they are doing.

Routes to Market

How will you sell your product or service? Through a retail outlet, online, to other businesses, via wholesalers and distributors? Think about how you will get whatever it is you are selling out there into the world. Could you use an existing sales channel like Amazon or Etsy? Set up a stall at festivals? Advertise yourself on LinkedIn?

The Brand

I'd also add something in your business plan about the brand you are selling. Most businesses need a brand personality like The Beatles or Coca-Cola, and creating it should be an enjoyable part of the process. That brand can then do anything it wants. Red Bull is an energy drink, but it also now runs magazines, publishing companies, recording studios, TV stations and all sorts of things. In a small way, the *Idler* is a brand that can do whatever it likes: sell books, run courses or set up a hot-dog stall at a festival if it so chooses – just so long as we do not dilute our brand by taking on too much.

People buy into an attitude and a vibe. Look at punk: the music is often pretty average but it is the style of its delivery that holds the appeal. But remember: a brand does not appear overnight. A logo and a misspelt word do not make a brand. A brand is the personality of your business, and it will only be created over time.

The Context

Next, you need to think about the global picture, or what is sometimes called 'the context'. Are you going with the wider flow? What are the laws and regulations relating to your business? When Amazon started, I remember scoffing at it. In its first year or two, its revenues were about as much as those of a corner shop. But through a mixture of riding the wave as far as online shopping went and having an enormous pile of money, the business became a giant.

Sometimes, a business can enjoy an amazing stroke of luck. Luke Johnson tells the story of when he went into the casinos business. A few months after he did so, a new law reduced a tax on gambling, thereby increasing the revenues of the business by a healthy percentage overnight.

Research the area you want to go into. Right now, the fashion is for new companies to declare that they are going to 'disrupt' an existing industry, whether it be laundry, men's shirt-making, taxis or hotels. And the new company will research the industry it intends to disrupt. I would imagine that Uber knew, as they grew their freelance taxi business, that they would face protests from existing taxi set-ups and regulatory hurdles all over the world. So the company employed teams of top lawyers, lobbyists and PR experts, such as their spin doctor in Europe, Rachel Whetstone, who was formerly head of communications for Google in Europe.

Sadly, most of us are not funded by banks and venture capitalists so we cannot afford to employ spin doctors of the calibre and pedigree of Rachel Whetstone. So we must keep plugging on and being true to ourselves. In the case of the *Idler*, the context was a society plagued by rising levels of anxiety and stress, which we reckoned could be alleviated by enjoyable and witty learning resources, articles and videos.

The Financials

You will need to include some spreadsheets in your business plan.

The main one is something called a P&L forecast. I'll go into this in more detail in the next chapter; for the moment, it is enough to say that this is a prediction of the revenue you expect the business to create, the expenses you will incur and the resulting profit or loss over a given time frame. You may also need to provide a cash-flow forecast. This is a prediction of the movement of money in and out of your business.

When I wrote our first business plan, I spent hours doing a cash-flow forecast on Excel on the advice of Dan, who kindly sent me an example that he was using (you can also find useful templates and examples online). I never showed it to anyone important, i.e. someone with money, but it was an excellent exercise in being forced to think through the costs of our business. You must not forget any tiny detail: insurance, computers, phone, utility bills, council rates, and so on. These all add up to form your fixed costs, that is, the amount of money that will go out even if none at all comes in.

When you are starting out, this is an extremely useful exercise. In our case, when we had a shop, I calculated that it would cost something like £8,000 a month to run our business. That meant that, to make a margin of 50 per cent, we would have to turn over £16,000 each month in book and event sales in order to break even. (VAT should be stripped out.)

Enough for the moment. Let's move on to look at just one element of all this in more detail: the spreadsheet.

4. Learn to Love the Spreadsheet

Seest thou a man diligent in his business, he shall stand
before the kings.

— Proverbs xxi, 29

Bohemian types tend to feign indifference to matters of record-keeping. They don't like to be thought of as the kind of square who likes poring over columns of numbers. That feels Scrooge-like, anti-life, boring, dusty, bureaucratic. Bohemians want to get out there and live, lie on divans, smoke opium and discuss the short life and tragic death of Thomas Chatterton, boy poet.

We don't want to be bourgeois. We want to be artists, poets, musicians. We feel like Dustin Hoffman's Ben in *The Graduate*. We don't want to go into plastics. We want to take acid and dance round the bonfire in ecstatic oblivion with topless hippie chicks and chaps.

But I know from experience that neglect of record-keeping will lead to chaos and poverty, and then you'll have no money to be bohemian. You'll just be destitute and angry. Don't get me wrong: I'm no breadhead, man; I'm just saying that you need to be sensible when it comes to managing your financial affairs. And while it is obviously good advice that you should delegate this stuff, because it's good to delegate the stuff we're not good at, you should, ideally, understand it before you delegate it. Otherwise, you might end up like Sting or Hanif Kureishi, both of whom were taken to the cleaners by their accountants.

So, you need to acquaint yourself with some spreadsheet basics. To talk to accountants, you need to learn how to be an accountant.

Now, I'm not saying anything new here. Even Socrates, the original bohemian, seemed to think it was wise to keep things tidy. The earliest economics textbook is generally considered to be the fourth-century *Oeconomicus* of Xenophon. It is a guide to running an ordered household and is in the form of conversations between Socrates and a young man called Critobulus, and later with a well-known Athenian, Ischomachus.

In his questioning style, Socrates asserts that managing a business or a household is a science: 'Is estate management the name of a branch of knowledge, like medicine, smithing and carpentry?' Here we have the suggestion that Socrates – who went around without shoes, did not earn money and has the reputation of being something of an anti-consumerist (after all, he is supposed to have said, 'What a lot of things are here that I don't need!' on entering the marketplace) considered the prudent management of the household to be a matter of great importance when pursuing the good life.

We can be fairly sure that his expert authority, Ischomachus, would have been au fait with spreadsheets, had they been available in ancient Athens. As it was, he probably got a slave to do the accounts. But he would have kept a close eye on the slave. As I do now with my accounts slave, Frank.

Ischomachus in this book says that order is beautiful, citing the example of a well-organized ship he once visited. 'Order saves time' is the idea here. Efficiency is the brother of leisure: 'I noticed that each kind of thing was so neatly stowed away that there was no confusion, no work for a searcher, nothing out of place, no troublesome untying to cause delay when anything was wanted for immediate use.' If you are anything like me, and tend towards throwing things in a heap, you'll know how good this advice is. I have wasted so much time and energy looking in a panic for hastily discarded car keys.

It may sound anti-bohemian, but Ischomachus sees beauty in order: 'What a beautiful sight is afforded by boots of all sorts and conditions ranged in rows ... Yes, no serious man will smile when I claim that there is beauty even in the order of pots and pans set out in neat array, however much it may move the laughter of a wit.'

A spreadsheet is like this row of boots: neat, orderly and pleasing to the eye. And it can be easily used by other people.

So my message is: be an accountant. In the eighteenth century and earlier, rudimentary book-keeping was considered to be an essential part of the education of children. This is because it was a pre-job age, in a sense. More people were self-employed and there was less protection from the state. So it behoved us all to make good accounts, whether in the household or in business. Now things are heading back in that direction: large companies are shedding jobs and individuals are seeking a number of clients rather than a full-time job. Self-employment is on the rise. Fewer of us in the future will be sucking at the teat of big business and big government. So we need to grow up and do, or at least understand, our own books.

And this need not be a burden. In fact, doing the books can be a calming and enjoyable process. I personally have struggled with laziness and chaos all my life. That's why I was attracted to the work of Dr Johnson, who wrote the original *Idler* columns. He was very talented and very productive but found it difficult to get out of bed in the morning. To calm his brain, he enjoyed making calculations and doing the accounts for friends' businesses; in addition, he would often be found conducting chemistry experiments in his bedroom.

I find the same. I enjoy doing figures and trying to get things in order on the backs of envelopes. And if you can treat spreadsheets in the same way that an artist treats his work, then you can even draw creative satisfaction from them, make them both beautiful and useful.

Your financial affairs are a bit like a garden: it is far preferable to do a little bit every day than catch up occasionally. I did not keep a proper eye on the books at the *Idler* for the first couple of years, and the result was that our accountant had to spend a week doing hours of detective work trying to figure out what had actually been going on in advance of filing our annual return. The result was a mighty bill. And I had to help, trying to remember why I had visited a cashpoint machine and withdrawn fifty pounds on 12 April 2013. Now, after many false starts, we have found an excellent book-keeper to keep us on track. She is saving me a ton of stress.

Spreadsheets are Beautiful

For years, I feared the spreadsheet. I feared its rigour and unbending loyalty to its own rules. I was too lazy to figure out how to use one. I scribbled columns of figures on the backs of envelopes, which I then lost.

One day, though, my accountant said, 'The spreadsheet is a thing of great beauty.' He loved the order behind them, and also the way that one small change – a slight adjustment to one figure, one cell – would ripple through the rest of the spreadsheet, magically changing all the numbers at a keystroke.

You may think that you simply don't have the time to learn how to do this. You are a bustling entrepreneur and your time would better be spent on creative projects and selling your wares. *Make the time.* Spend an evening with a spreadsheet program and a bottle of wine or a couple of bottles of real ale.

A spreadsheet is a lattice or grid of numbered rows and columns. Along the top, the columns are labelled alphabetically and, down the side, they are numbered. Each box is called a cell, and a cell can contain a number, a letter, a word or a formula. A cell is referred to, in chess-like manner, by its letter and number, for example, B46 or H2.

The first spreadsheet was invented by a computer geek

in 1979 and was given the name VisiCalc. The term 'spread-sheet' derives from traditional book-keeping practice, where items were named, itemized, listed and added up in columns. When an error was made, related entries had to be redone by hand. With the magical spreadsheet, every figure will correct itself. You can also speculate and fantasize and see what happens when you put in different figures.

Yes, spreadsheets can be fun.

First Steps with Spreadsheets

As a good bohemian, you may hate and loathe the global ad-sales business called Google. It is too big.

But Google does great things, and one of them is Google Drive. With this cloud-based file-sharing system, you can make spreadsheets, presentations and word-processing documents and work on them with your staff, or 'team', as the modern parlance has it. I would recommend opening a Google account, going to 'sheets' and starting to play around.

It would also be sensible and wise to invite a friend over who has some experience in spreadsheets. Screen-learning is one thing, but learning from a human being is better.

I would also advise a third teacher, and that is a book. Keep a good book to hand. I'll be going into basic accounting in more depth in the next chapter. For now, I just want to get across the idea that you must take responsibility for your own accounting. Your spouse will not do it for you. Your book-keeper will not do it for you. Your accountant will not do it for you. Your business partner – at least at the beginning – will not do it for you either. You must take on the basics yourself. You must take responsibility, and the spreadsheet will help you.

So go ahead. Open a Google Sheet. You'll see a nice empty grid, just waiting to be filled in. It will look like this:

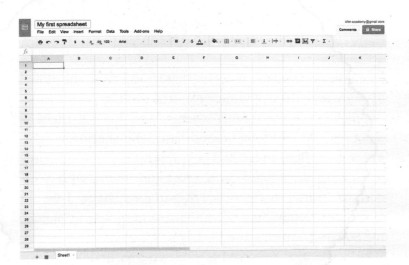

You see a network of boxes. Each one is a cell. Go, for example, to C3. Write a title into it, something like 'Outgoings. August 2016.' Now write some headings across the top, for example, the names of the calendar months. On the left, write 'Sales'. Then under that, write out your different sources of revenue. When you've done a few, write 'Total' on the line below.

The spreadsheet will automatically add all the numbers in a column if you ask it to. Click in the cell under all the figures, and go to the top of the page, where you will see a strange E-like character. You are aiming to add up every figure in the 'Amount' column. This is fairly straightforwardly done. Let us say that the 'Amount' is column E. In the 'Total' cell, you'll want a formula like this: SUM(D3:D15). That will add up everything from D3 to D15. If you want to add the amounts written in discrete cells together, you separate the cells with semicolons, for example, SUM(D3;D15;D14). You can put whatever sum or formula you like in the cell. It could be a simple sum or a complicated one.

You could also try another useful exercise: overheads. Overheads are the monthly outgoings that you cannot avoid paying, whatever you do and whatever state your business happens to be in. They are also called fixed costs or running costs. They do not include the cost of buying stock or making your product. In our case, they are wages, rent, rates, electricity, phone, the internet, computers, insurance, utility bills and cleaning. We would have to pay these costs even if we sold nothing in a month.

Sit down and make a spreadsheet of your fixed costs. This was a great bit of advice that was given to me by Tom, the architect who designed our bookshelves at the Idler Academy. It's a simple spreadsheet that includes a SUM cell, which automatically adds up all the figures in the column.

Now I'd like to tell you about a term that you will hear a lot in business: 'P&L'. I remember being in a meeting with a festival organizer, nice bloke called Jim. We agreed a plan, and then he said, 'Right, we'll do a P&L,' as if it was the most natural thing in the world to say.

Victoria and I had absolutely no idea what he was talking about.

Well, P&L is profit and loss. And here is a definition from a financial dictionary: 'A financial statement that summarizes the revenues, costs, and expenses incurred during a specific period, usually a fiscal quarter or a year. P&L statements provide information that shows the ability of a company to generate profit by increasing revenue and reducing costs; it also is known as a statement of profit and loss, an income statement, or an income and expense statement.'

You can also do a P&L for a specific product. We do them for our events. We have a great spreadsheet on our Googledocs which lists how many tickets have been sold, along with the name, email address and telephone number of each customer. We have set the document up so that the total revenue is displayed, along with the costs incurred in staging the event – speaker fees, venue hire, staff costs, buying drink to sell on, and so on. An adjustment is made for VAT to give a net figure. The profit or loss is then calculated as the net figure minus the costs.

This system means we can monitor in real time how each event is doing, and we can also look back at old events and see which ones made money and how we organized these money-making ones. It also helps us, as the august definition above suggests, to reduce costs and increase revenue on each event. A small decrease in costs and a small increase in revenues could change an entire event, or the launch of a particular product, from being a loss-making disaster into an enjoyable and profitable project.

In the next chapter, we are going to look at a few basics of book-keeping and accounting, in order to dissipate any residual fear you may have around numbers.

5. The Art of Accounting

I must create a system or be enslaved by another man's; I
will not reason and compare: my business is to create.

— William Blake

Now that you have a nodding acquaintance with the spreadsheet and have lost your fear of this very useful tool and friend to the businesslike bohemian, it is time to move on to the art of accounting. I call it an 'art' because the best way to enjoy accounting is to treat it as such. Approach accounting as you would the design of a new product: Do it well, do it carefully, do it beautifully.

On our Business for Bohemians course, we run a session with a wonderful accountant called Emily Coltman. Emily is our accounting guru. She is high up at an accounting software company called Freeagent. Her sessions, weirdly, are the most fun and lively of all the business lessons we hold. Emily says that accounting is a creative art: give two accountants the same data and they will come up with different accounts. Now, it takes years to get an accountancy qualification, so I do not promise anything like full training in this chapter. I just want to outline a few principles.

Take Responsibility

As the founder of and possibly the only person involved in this business, you will need to take responsibility for the accounts. You will have to learn a little rudimentary book-keeping. It is a great shame that book-keeping is not taught as a matter of course in schools, as it was in the eighteenth century, before we all became slaves in the mills. All children should be taught the basics of double entry, in my view.

When it comes to accounting, do not, as I did, do it in a terrific hurry at midnight, on your knees, with the floor of your room covered in piles of papers. You still need to get help to do your books and accounts – but you need to make sure you are involved and understand what is happening.

To be successful in business, you not only need to understand accounting, you need to *be* an accountant. Again and again, while looking into the business world, I have seen that entrepreneurs are usually accountants. The founders of Innocent Smoothies were not hippies with a festival stall. They were trained accountants with an idea. James Daunt of Daunt Books was not originally a book-seller. He was an accountant. As was Tim Waterstone of Waterstones.

And you have to recognize that accounting is an ongoing process. When I was a freelance journalist, I saw accounting as something that had to be done only once a year, when it was time to send in my tax return. I'm afraid that I carried over a bit of this attitude when Victoria and I started our Academy project. However, accounts are, in fact, the lifeblood of your business. You will not be able to make good decisions unless you know what is going on with the figures, or, I should say, with the data.

The first step should be to get some advice from a friend. Go and see a well-organized one and ask them how they manage their books and accounts and whether they could recommend an accountant. But before you talk to them, it would pay to study the subject a little bit. At least get your head around the terminology. That is where I can help.

Different Kinds of Accounting

The first thing to realize about the art of accounting is that book-keeping, accountancy and management accountancy are different things. Book-keeping is about keeping good records of what is going in and out of your business. Most businesses hire a book-keeper to pop in when required and prepare the books for the accountant, who is the one who will do your tax return.

But do not make the mistake I did and assume that everything is going swimmingly. I'm afraid to report that I singularly failed to keep our book-keeper in check for the first three years or so. He came in occasionally, sat down with some files, left and sent us an invoice. When it came to doing the VAT returns, I would get an email like this: 'The VAT return was due yesterday. Please can I have your income and expenditure details for the period?'

Hang on: I thought I was paying you to do that? You want this yesterday? That means we have already missed the deadline and will have to pay a fine. The chaotic system, and my attempt to delegate the book-keeping, caused all kinds of headaches for me. It was me, after all, as the director, who had to call up what is generally a terrifying Scottish woman with a voice like Miss Jean Brodie to ask for more time to pay what we owed, and our fines.

To avoid the scrape I got myself in, I would advise you to learn the basics. I realize now that you need to employ a book-keeper to come in regularly – at least once a month, and preferably weekly if you are doing over a hundred transactions a week – and that you should sit down with them while they are in the office (or beach café, or canal boat, or other nomadic location).

Next, what is an accountant? An accountant is a qualified professional who prepares official accounts and sends your tax returns in to the government each year. If you are a sole trader, this is a fairly straightforward process: money in, money out, profit (if any); you pay tax on that profit. An accountant provides a historical record of what happened during a given period. You may in fact only be given the accounts for a certain twelve-month period six months or more after that period has elapsed.

If you are a partnership or a limited company, you have to send proper accounts back to the government which show your income, outgoings, profit and a balance sheet, which gives a snapshot of the assets and liabilities of your company. The balance sheet also describes how shares have been distributed and how much money has been invested. It is worth trying to understand how the balance sheet works.

I remember asking the bank for an overdraft and the spotty Herbert on the other end of the phone said, 'I don't like the look of your balance sheet.' I had absolutely no idea what he was talking about.

Company Accounts: A Brief Introduction

Now, I'm going to take you through a set of company accounts page by page and explain what it all means. It doesn't matter if you are a sole trader and don't see this as being relevant to you. It will all help in the journey towards being businesslike and in control of your finances. Being in control will save you money: it is when we hide our heads in the sand that the banks and tax-collectors start piling on the fines.

Take note of this first line: you generally do your accounts for a period of twelve months, and it's up to you in which month your accounting year begins and ends. For some strange reason, the financial year in the UK runs from April to April, but you can set your own financial year to begin at any time.

Profit and Loss Account for the Year Ended
31 August 2014

1. Turnover: all the money that came in (e.g. £200,000)
2. Cost of sales: the money you spent on stock, product development, marketing, printing, fees to freelancers and contributors, etc. (e.g. £75,000)
3. Gross profit: turnover minus cost of sales (e.g. £125,000)
4. Administrative expenses or fixed costs (overheads): cost of office, staff, heating, etc. (e.g. £100,000)
5. Operating profit or loss is turnover minus cost of sales minus administrative expenses or fixed costs (e.g. £200,000 − £75,000 − £100, 000), so here, £25,000

Well done. You made a profit of £25,000 that year.

A note on gross profit: this is the money made on sales before the overheads are taken into account. For example, if the ingredients of a pizza, the dough, sauce, cheese and other toppings cost £1 and the pizza is sold for £10, the gross profit is £9. In percentage terms, the gross profit margin is 90 per cent.

Next we move on to the balance sheet, which, on first sight, looks horrific. I confess that I didn't look at ours for years. The bare minimum had been done, in that we had got our accounts to Companies House, the government-run control centre for all businesses, and our tax return to

HMRC. That was enough for me. Mistake! I would recommend that you go through the accounts with the
accountant line by line. Ask them to explain everything.
This seems like a tedious process, and it may in fact be
quite painful, but it will be worth it.

The assets part of your balance sheet will list fixed
assets, current assets and creditors. A fixed asset is something the company owns which has value, like a machine
or a property. Next come current assets. This is a list of all
your assets which could be converted into cash if required.
In our case, it would be our stock of books and gifts. Current assets also includes how much you are owed and how
much cash you have in the bank. Under 'Creditors' come
your liabilities: in other words, what you owe. This
includes bank loans, tax debts and loans taken out from
individuals or other businesses.

Next on the balance sheet is the heading 'Total assets
less current liabilities'. In our case, looking at the accounts
for our first two years, this was anything from twenty to
forty grand – in brackets. Brackets are bad! They mean a
loss. Therefore, our balance sheet, that is, the document
showing what we own, showed that not only did we not
own anything but we owed a lot.

OK, I can sense that your eyes are glazing over. But I
hope I have got my point across. To reiterate that point
once more: as the business owner, you need both to take
responsibility for your accounts and, at the same time, to
delegate them.

System, System, System

One of my favourite songs is 'Systematic Death' by punk band Crass. It's the story of an ordinary middle-class couple who are trapped by the 'system'. They work in boring jobs, never express themselves freely and then, when it is time to retire and their mortgage is almost paid off, they die. It's a very tragic story, and it inspired me to name an issue of the *Idler* 'Smash the System'.

However, when it comes to your accounting, you absolutely must have a system. Otherwise, you are going to be wandering around in a daze and making decisions based on vague impressions rather than actual figures. You can create your own system, but everyone you work with must be trained in it. Your staff must also enslave themselves to this system. So get them to help in creating it so that they feel a part of it.

I can tell you that running an anti-capitalist, anti-consumerist business has presented some challenges. In the early days, staff were attracted to our shop by a perceived *Idler* ethos and seemed mildly put out that they were expected to work in return for their fifty quid a day. They didn't expect to have to vacuum the floor, clean the loo, move furniture around and generally do what they were told.

I had to put a sign on the wall in the kitchen which read: 'No idling'. Not that it made any difference. When Victoria and I were away, they'd sit in the basement smoking weed and drinking our wine. *Mea culpa*, I guess.

Invoices

You need to create an invoice template for sending out invoices. There are loads online. Suffice it to say that it will need your address, your bank account details and your payment terms. For the terms, write 'immediate payment'. If you write 'thirty days', they will not pay you for *at least* thirty days. Getting paid can be difficult for small businesses (we'll come back to that). You'll need to make a list of when you sent your invoices and note down when they are paid. There are loads of programs and enterprises out there that will help you do this.

You'll also need a list of the invoices you have received, when they were received and when they were paid. If you receive invoices in the mail, before they are dealt with they need to be hole punched and placed in a large ring binder labelled 'Unpaid Invoices'. The invoice category – books, stationery, motor expenses, repairs, etc. – must be noted somehow on the invoice. When it has been paid, write the date of payment on it and move it to a different-coloured ring binder labelled 'Paid Invoices'.

We keep a Googlesheet record of all invoices received and when they are paid. The bohemian in business might do better to sign up with an online accounting company. They have invented great systems so you don't have to, or use Quick Books. Or otherwise employ a book-keeper one day a month. Outsource, my friends!

The Wonders of Googledrive

At the *Idler* we put our various lists of what we owe on a Googledoc. This means that we can all look at it wherever we are. At this precise moment, for example, I am sitting in the library room of my local community theatre. Victoria and Julian, the manager, are in the shop. Bobbie, our events manager, is at Glastonbury. But we can all look at what we owe right now. I can also access the company bank account from wherever I am.

When it comes to the company bank account, you should inspect it daily, particularly if you have a business like ours, which is quite complicated, with between five and twenty sales each day. If you're a consultant sending out one invoice a month, then, clearly, your book-keeping will not be so complicated and you will not need to check every day.

With the help of your book-keeper, set up a decent system. It would pay to meet the book-keeper frequently when you are setting things up and to work with them very closely. As time moves on, you'll be able to let them get on with it.

The Importance of Management Accounts

Let me say a few words now about management accounts. 'Do your management accounts' is one of John Brown's top bits of business advice. And I have to confess that, until a couple of months ago, I had not even heard of management accounts. He scoffed and laughed at me when I admitted this. 'Don't you want to know what's going on in your own business?' he snorted.

Management accounts are the detailed accounts that should be done every month so that you can check how your business is doing. John showed me an account for February. It looked like this:

		Actual	Budget	Variance
Tombo Books Ltd				
Profit and Loss Budget Performance: Feb				
2016-02-01				
Sales		116768	108492	8276
Cost of Goods		72911	64339	8572
Gross profit		43857	44153	8572
Overheads				
	Wages	15761	13900	1861
	Office	3148	3200	-52
	Accounts	1000	1000	0
	Travel	500	250	250
	TOTAL	20409	18350	2059
Profit		23448	25803	6513

This simple spreadsheet shows what sales were made in February and what they cost the business. There are two types of cost: the cost of the actual materials (e.g. flour for bread), called 'cost of goods', and the costs incurred every month to run things – wages, rent, fees, and so on, called 'overheads'. To get the gross profit, you subtract cost of goods from sales. To get the net profit, you subtract the overheads from the gross profit.

In management accounts, you compare what actually happened (actual) with what you predicted would happen (budget). Then you see the variance, either up or down. You must produce something like this during the first week of every month.

You must, must, must set up a management accounting system if your business does more than a handful of transactions each month.

As the anonymous author of *The Rural Socrates*, an American estate-management manual from 1800, puts it, when detailing the advice he gave to a farmer:

> I instructed him in the method of keeping regular accounts of his receipts and expenses; and recommended sending one of his sons to learn writing and arithmetic; nor had I any difficulty in making him comprehend, that by particularizing every part of labor, expence and profit, and marking the progress and minute circumstances which attended his improvements, he would be much better enabled to form a precise and adequate judgement of their value; while the wisest man may suffer himself to be deceived as well as deceive others, if he trusts to the uncertainty and deceitfulness of memory.

Oh, how often, I wonder, have I deceived myself about aspects of our business by trusting to my impressions rather than looking at the cold, hard facts!

Well, the key points about management accounts are budget and variance. Again, John Brown was appalled that I did not know what either 'budget' or 'variance' meant. But now I do. Budget is your forecast for that month's revenues and outgoings. Actual budget is what you actually do. And variance is the difference between the two.

Why is this important? Well, because it helps the business owner – that's you! – make plans to reduce working in some areas, increase in other ones, to decide what is working and what is not. The process of doing this forces you to create targets and to think through every detail of your operation.

If you don't have management accounts, then you are lost in a fog of your own creation, which is what happened to Victoria and me in the first three years. We were so busy firefighting (or, 'shouting'), as the process of every-day crisis management is called, there seemed to be precious little time left over to monitor the book-keeping, let alone create management accounts.

Pay Your Taxes, or Else

While we're on this sort of thing, can I add a note? You will find that HMRC does not react kindly to not being paid VAT or PAYE, preferably, on time. If you can't pay it in one lump sum now, then give them a call and work out a repayment scheme. I've done this twice and the terrifying-sounding Scottish woman will generally help you to avoid going bankrupt. It is also better to pay a small amount towards your debt than to pay nothing at all.

Above all, you, as the owner of a company, must know what is going on in that company. This will relieve stress; it will not create it. What *is* stressful is to wander around in a muddle and make decisions based on fear, panic and vague impressions rather than on the figures, on the actual financial state of your business.

You never know: the real figures may paint a more positive picture than you anticipate when you are lying in bed, staring at the ceiling in a state of high anxiety, at 5 o'clock in the morning. Consider using an online accounting service such as Freeagent, at which, as I mentioned, our accounting teacher, Emily, works. There are plenty of these around, and I wish we'd used one five years ago.

Knowledge is Power

One day when I was in the shop a harassed middle-aged man came in and asked me whether I knew how much was being asked for in rent for the empty restaurant down the road. It turned out that he owned two pubs. We chatted for a while, and he gave me two pieces of advice: 'Never, ever look at the accounts' and 'Just . . . keep . . . going.'

The first is clearly a bad idea, unless you are made of sterner stuff than I am. There are some entrepreneurs out there who genuinely don't seem to care if they plunge into debt and have the bailiffs knocking. They just move on, go bankrupt, pop up somewhere else. I think the problem with your bohemian types is that they are likely to be sensitive and acutely aware of how other people feel. So they may not have the really thick skin of Philip Green, Rupert Murdoch, Richard Branson and other big capitalists.

The second bit, though, 'Just keep going', is excellent advice, and forgive me for repeating it. If you genuinely believe that what you are doing is a good thing, then you should just keep going, even if you are not reaping proper dividends. Find some other way of paying for your daily bread. James Dyson worked on his vacuum cleaners for seventeen years before his business took off. His children had all left home and had grown up in poverty – or, at least, in very modest circumstances. The Dysons lived on the money Mrs Dyson made as an art teacher. But he kept going. So it is for me and the *Idler*: I would keep going for ever, whether the business made money or not, because it is my vocation.

The other reason to keep going is that you never know what is going to turn up. Something may change in society at large. You may be lucky. A spotlight may be turned on you.

It is also true, I think, that the longer you keep going, the more trustworthy you will become and the more people will want to invest money in your business. No one wants to invest in an idea. They want to invest in people. But make a start, trade for five years, don't go out of business, and a potential backer might have confidence in you. It's also worth remembering that a business can take a long, long, long time to get anywhere. Luke Johnson told us that a business takes five to ten years to establish itself.

A final word on accounting: buy a good book, an introduction to book-keeping. I, personally, like Emily Coltman's books. Or try *Book-keeping for Dummies*. Books provide a far easier and more effective way to learn than Googling. I know, I've tried both. There is a lot of rubbish out there on the web, and it's impossible for the beginner to sort the wheat from the chaff. The author of a real book has done that work for you, plus you can stuff a book in your pocket and read it in bed without burning your chest off with laptop heat.

6. Get the Price Right and Get Paid

Price is often taken as an indication of quality. I have friends who automatically go for the most expensive alternative on the assumption that it is likely to be the best.
— Charles Handy

Pricing is a tricky issue. Your instinct when starting a business is to set your prices too low, because, as a good bohemian, you want to be nice and fair. I used to make this mistake. I priced our events too low and I was too generous with contributors. Mistake. Low prices are for giant companies. Small companies need to charge high prices.

I learned the hard way. I liked the idea of charging £10 per ticket for an evening talk and paying the speaker £200. What would happen was this: we would get thirty people. That's £300. Pay VAT and the speaker fee and you have made a gross profit of £50. Hopeless.

There is a personality problem here: when I get money, I have a terrible urge to get rid of it immediately, either by paying someone else or by spending it. I am over-generous. This is perhaps a positive quality, but an excess of it is foolhardy. So I have learned to rein in these tendencies.

Do not sell cheap. One year at a festival we ran a bacon-butties stall to try to make some extra cash. We undercut the other bacon-butty stalls there. We sold a lot of bacon butties but, in the end, made virtually no money after we'd taken into account all our costs (and that was with me paying myself £0).

We made two basic business errors: first, we worked our arses off just to break even. And second, we undercut the other stalls, which makes us scumbags and no better than Amazon. In bohemian business, you should never undercut your competitors. We are not Uber or Amazon. Those companies are brutal and wrong.

After a while, you realize that a price that is too low benefits no one except the punter. No one will get paid, you'll be dipping into your credit card to pay your VAT bill, you won't be able to pay staff and your direct debit to the council for your business rates will bounce. But at least, for a moment, a few people thought your product or service was relatively cheap.

Charlie Gladstone is a creative entrepreneur I really admire. The great-grandson of William Gladstone, he runs a real-life and online shop called Pedlars and founded a small festival called the Good Life Experience. I asked him for some business advice, and he stressed the importance of pricing. 'You have to understand margin,' he said. 'If you don't, you're stuffed ... understand pricing from day one – anyone can give stuff away.' Hark those words of wisdom!

Keep Your Prices High

So, whether you are selling a product or a service, you must start off with the highest price you can bear to charge. I met Serena Rees, the entrepreneur who created underwear brand Agent Provocateur. Her business is (or was: she and her partner sold it to the Chinese for some gigantic sum) selling knickers. But, really, her business is to buy very small pieces of material for nothing and then sell them at huge prices. It's a bit like crisps. Buy half a potato for three pence, slice it and fry it, put it in a shiny bag and sell it for sixty pence. That's a gross profit margin of 57/60 x 100, so 95 per cent. Anyway, Serena's advice as far as pricing goes is: 'Think of a price. Double it. Add VAT.'

It's the same at Rough Trade, the independent record-store chain. I worked there in the early nineties and noticed that their prices were kept very high. The indie-pop record buyers didn't seem to mind. As a small business, you cannot compete on price with the likes of Amazon, who have – completely unfairly – traded on tiny margins in order to get the sales in.

Records have lower margins than books. Rough Trade Records' Nigel House told us that he works on a profit margin of a third. That means that if he sells a CD for £15, he gets to keep £5. That is before the overheads like staff, rent, website, and so on, have been calculated, of course.

Think about prescription drugs. A tiny bottle of liquid,

which must have cost pennies to produce (yes, I know that there are research costs, but I'm talking about cost of goods here), retails for a tenner. No wonder GlaxoSmith-Kline's boss earns millions of pounds a year. The main point here is, why should you, a bohemian in business, undersell yourself? You may have to cope with whingers, but that is better than going bankrupt after three years.

The good thing about high prices is that you can always reduce them, or have a sale. We occasionally run a half-price sale on a product that we have already paid for, for example, calendars, *Idler* books or online courses. This raises cash and gets the product flowing, and it's fun, because we know that our products are getting out there.

First Steps

When setting prices, you should look at what your competitors are charging. When we launched our Idler Academy project, we looked at similar organizations, such as the School of Life, other ukulele courses, calligraphy, creative writing and gardening courses. We set our prices somewhere in the middle. They were higher than you'd pay at your local community college for a pottery evening class but lower than what a big organization such as the *Guardian* newspaper group was charging for its novel-writing workshops. Roughly speaking, the business we are in tends to charge punters something in the range of £100 to £250 a day for courses, and £40 to £50 for evening masterclasses.

We noticed that the *Guardian* was charging sky-high rates for similar offerings to ours: probably about twice as much. We should have followed suit, but I didn't have the nerve.

When producing the *Idler* magazine, we noticed that similar indie mags on offer had high cover prices between £10 and £15. We set our cover price at £9. The first thing a certain venture capitalist said to me when he saw it was: 'You're too cheap.'

We got the price right with our books. We produce a series called *Idler* Guides. These are short introductions to weighty subjects by great writers. They are a mere sixty-four pages. But we kept the price at £8.95, and they sold well.

One thing we realized is that 'free', when it comes to events, is a waste of time, because people don't bother turning up. 'Free' means crap. Every now and then, perhaps stricken by conscience, we put on a free event. In general, these are less busy than events we charge for. If you have not paid, you are less likely to leave the pub at the appointed time, particularly if the sun is shining, or you may just feel like taking a snooze.

We have also noticed that free events attract cranks. Victoria and I put on a free taster event to try to sell tickets to a business course. Twenty people came along for the free entertainment and free gin and tonics. It was a lovely evening, until one older chap piped up, 'This is all nonsense, isn't it? You can't do good-quality things and make money. Not in this philistine country.' I attempted to placate him and moved on swiftly to another punter.

After an hour, we started to wind up the event. The gent piped up again: 'Chucking us all out now, then, are you?'

Whatever you're selling, whether it's T-shirts, festival tickets, skateboards, your own time, coffee, American cereals, ice cream or letterpress bookmarks, keep the price high, but not so high, clearly, that no one buys what you do. My friend Jim, who runs various pop festivals in the UK, reckons that if people are complaining, then you've got the price about right.

Day Rates for Consultants

If you are a consultant, then you need to set a day rate. Again, I would recommend looking at what people in a similar profession with a similar level of experience are charging. And, again, be wary of underselling yourself. People stuck in corporations or bureaucracies often complain that their organization is paying outsiders £1,000 a day. But these consultants may only get the occasional day at that rate. The rest of their time is spent pitching, researching, preparing, working on their website, selling and marketing.

The day rates that people charge can look steep. Young techies can charge something in the region of £100 to £150 a day. Our web company charges us between £700 and £800 a day. A teaching firm we use for our business courses charges £250 a day. Proofreaders charge £180 per day. And independent business consultants can charge more.

So, as a consultant, I would set your rate as high as you

can bear. If you get it wrong, it doesn't matter: it is easier to come down than to go up. And what you are trying to do as a consultant is to reduce the headaches for your client, take some work off their hands or increase their sales in some way, one hopes for ever. So, as far as they are concerned, your high day rate will be worth it.

An alternative would be to examine a retainer model – that is, a contract whereby your clients pay in advance for work that will be specified later. Find several clients and charge them each something like £700 a month.

In the late nineties, my friend Gavin Pretor-Pinney and I ran a creative consultancy working for big companies (which was certainly my most successful business ever, in financial terms). We charged £1,000 a day for our combined efforts, plus the efforts of Dan Kieran, our number three. When working out a budget for a job, we'd calculate how many days it would take us to do the work and multiplied it by a thousand. We charged for about two hundred and fifty days a year. That way, we covered our very low overheads (office rent, Dan, computers), supported the *Idler* magazine (still a non-profit, though not by design) and made a profit of £200,000 a year.

Virtual Product Pricing

Our idea with online courses was to produce a fun, educational experience in video form. My own course, How to be Idle, consists, of six half-hour lectures. If written down, that amount of content would be about thirty thousand words;

that's half a short book. You can watch these films whenever you like, as often as you like. With them, you also get notes and access to forums. We wanted these online courses to be a democratic means of teaching which could be accessed all over the world. So we priced them at the same level as an expensive hardback book – in the region of £15 to £40. Anything less than that, and I reckon they would not be so highly valued by the consumer. They cost us anything from £2,000 to £5,000 to make. So, rather like a book, once you have sold a certain number, you start to make a profit.

When it comes to pricing a talk as an event, you are aiming for a price that will sell all the tickets on the last day. That, to me, means you have got it exactly right. Set the price too low, and you will sell out too quickly. Sell too high, and you'll be left with empty seats.

Bobbie, who used to work at the *Idler*, introduced a tiered system. We will sell a certain number of tickets at a low price, and the price will then increase slightly. The first few tickets are called 'early bird'. As the day approaches, we might introduce a third, and even a fourth, higher price. There are some people out there for whom it is not really an issue whether a ticket costs £20, £25 or £30. If they want to go to the event, they will pay.

Other people will be put off by a lower price. So we hope that, by using this three-tiered structure, we will sell all the tickets at the right price to the appropriate consumer. We adopted this approach most successfully with our Michael Palin event: the ticket price doubled across the four months they were on sale, and we almost exactly sold out on the day of the event.

Choosing Your Payment Systems

If you are taking more than a few payments each month, then you'll need some sort of 'payment gateway': a system of taking payments via the Internet.

For the very small business, it is fairly easy to set up an account with PayPal. This is the gigantic Silicon Valley success story which processes payments and takes a cut on every transaction. Quite a large cut, as it happens. With PayPal, your customers can pay from their PayPal account or with a debit card.

PayPal works, but it is expensive to use. Their commission on each transaction is 3.4 per cent plus twenty pence for each transaction. So if you sell a ticket or a book for £20, PayPal takes eighty-eight pence – that's nearly 5 per cent. Compare that to the 1.9 per cent charged by the debit- and credit-card companies.

We used PayPal exclusively for three years. Our next step was to install a more professional payment system, and we employed a web agency to help us to do this. Getting a professional-looking credit- and debit-card payment facility on your website is not as easy as you might think. When I applied for one, I was told by the bank, 'The underwriters don't like it.' This is because there was a risk associated with putting on events: there was a gap in time between the ticket going on sale for an event and the event actually taking place. During this time, the event could be cancelled and the customer would be due a refund. If we did not pay the refund, then the credit-card company would be liable. This is why they were reluctant to offer the service.

I didn't know what to do next. I ranted and raved. Then Victoria forwarded me an email from a specialist card-payment broker called Acceptcards. They were fantastic. They act like an insurance broker, as an intermediary between the business and the credit-card company. We rang them up and they sorted everything out for us. Once we'd set up this system, our sales went up.

Now, speaking of sales, how do you get them? What are they? Well, the first thing to understand about being a bohemian in business is that you are a salesperson. You are the communicator of an idea and, if people like it, they will give you money. And that is the subject of our next chapter.

7. How to Sell

If you can't smile, don't open a shop.
                                    – Chinese proverb

Uncomfortable though it may make you feel as a bohemian who floats above the sordid business of commerce, when you are self-employed, or running a small business, you are a salesperson. You are a market trader, crying, 'Come and get my lovely bananas!' You are a pedlar, a petit-bourgeois shopkeeper. Things do not, very sadly, sell themselves.

That goes for writers, photographers, artists, film-makers, woodworkers, hand-knitted-gift makers, wedding-service providers, window cleaners, locksmiths or whoever. Those of us who have ambitions to retain some autonomy over our working life and use our own creativity must, to an extent, out ourselves in the role of salesperson.

In the case of the bohemian in business, our sales technique may simply be the way we live and act. Successful artists and pop stars emanate a vibe and an attitude that people want to buy into: think of David Bowie and Damien Hirst.

Things for us mere mortals who seek autonomy,

though, are tougher than ever. When I published my first book, *How to be Idle*, in 2004, I did not lift a finger to promote it. The publisher did everything. These days, by contrast, when presenting a pitch for a book, you need to provide a marketing plan and promise to sell your butt off when the book is published. You have to get out there and hustle.

It would be easy to grumble about this – to think that it all seems so beneath you. But this aristocratic contempt of the lowly tradesman will get you nowhere. And aristocratic contempt for trade is itself absurd. For the aristos, whose ancestors were royal lickspittles, murderers, thieves and rascals, to look down on those who choose to open a shop and sell stuff is patently ridiculous. It's all right for the aristos to be anti-materialistic and to scorn trade when they own 20,000 acres and have a ton of serfs paying them rent every month. Does that give them the moral high ground? No.

The haughty prejudice against trade is not new: Cicero reported that the ancient Germanic warriors despised shopkeepers as lazy and spiritless. They decided it was more manly to kill, rape and steal than weigh out corn every day.

Anyway, it's easy to affect disdain for Mammon when you have millions of pounds coming in every year from renting out the land and property your forefathers were given for being flunkeys to Henry VIII. The Duke of Westminster probably finds trade a trifle vulgar.

What total bastards.

The aristos were not the only ones, though. Communism

was also prejudiced against entrepreneurs, even against writers and artists. Lenin despised small business and saw anarchists as bourgeois in disguise. Here is the Russian lunatic ranting against careerist writers and imagining the creation of a pure, clean Party literature written by the people: 'In contradistinction to bourgeois customs, to the profit-making, commercialized bourgeois press, to bourgeois literary careerism and individualism, "aristocratic anarchism" and drive for profit, the socialist proletariat must put forward the principle of Party literature . . . down with literary supermen!'

He goes on to assert that writers who are paid are no better than grubby shopkeepers: 'Emerging from the captivity of the feudal censorship, we have no desire to become, and shall not become, prisoners of bourgeois-shopkeeper literary relations. We want to establish, and we shall establish, a free press, free not simply from the police, but also from capital, from careerism, and what is more, free from bourgeois-anarchist individualism.'

As a shopkeeper and a writer, and a bourgeois-anarchist individualist, I feel doubly – nay, triply – affronted by Lenin's snobbery. It is actually only through becoming a shopkeeper, in the sense of making or buying stuff and then selling it, that we can find freedom. We will never find it by becoming subservient to a one-party socialist state or to a large corporation. Even if you enjoy a good salary, working for a large company or state is horribly restrictive. Luke Johnson tells me that he has noticed at dinner parties that the top lawyers and people who work in the City are not happy. They may be earning millions but, says Luke, 'It's just posh slavery.' They are tethered to their master. The financial rewards may be great, but what about their every-day life? It is misery with very long hours.

A nation of shopkeepers, as Napoleon never said, is a very beautiful thing to be. Before the Reformation in England in the sixteenth century, we were a proud country of yeomen, that is, small farmers and small business-people. And that is still an aspiration that is held dear across the world: to have your own shop, or farm. I have done both, and I can testify that the sense of freedom is palpable and that you will never be bored.

Now, though they do not look it at first sight, the petite bourgeoisie are the true revolutionaries. They are the ones who take the risk and open the shop. They start the small business. They are not content to follow the path of professional or employee. They are the anarchists, the ones who take responsibility, the ones who do not allow themselves to shift the blame on to boss or state.

We business bohemians do not moan. We act.

This is the view of James C. Scott, Sterling Professor of Political Science at Yale. In his essential collection of essays *Two Cheers for Anarchism* (a rather cautious title for what is a great book), Scott argues that it's the petite bourgeoisie who are the true anarchists: 'I believe that the petite bourgeoisie and small property in general represent a precious zone of autonomy and freedom in state systems increasingly dominated by large public and private bureaucracies. Autonomy and freedom are, along with mutuality, at the centre of an anarchist sensibility.' Not only that, but there are a lot of us. Scott suggests that the petite bourgeoisie possibly represents the largest social class in the world, numbering the following in its embrace: 'Small-holding peasants, artisans, pedlars, small independent professionals, and small traders ... tenant farmers, ploughmen with a draft animal, rag pickers and itinerant market women.' And those who are trapped in boring jobs, he says, dream of joining this class, precarious though it might be: 'The desire for autonomy, for control over the working day and the sense of freedom and self-respect such control provides, is a vastly underestimated social aspiration for much of the world's population.'

Trying to carve out some sort of freedom is certainly not an easy path; hence this book, which is designed to help people explore this approach to life with their eyes wide open.

Selling is Fun

One of the very nice things that happened when we opened our bookshop is that I learned how much I enjoyed selling books. The process of talking to a customer, chatting about books, advising them and seeing them walk out with a great work like *The Making of the English Working Class* by E. P. Thompson is satisfying indeed. It is education in action.

I realized that selling is not so different from my work as a journalist. Both involve getting enthusiastic about something and communicating that enthusiasm to a wider audience – and getting paid for it. It's about education. And it is easy to sell something which you genuinely like and are excited about.

But selling can also be dispiriting. Sometimes, I would be sitting at the till in an empty shop. Sometimes, a customer would wander in and, often, they would be a fan of my books. They would tell me how much they had enjoyed them, and then talk about their own lives for an hour or so. I would start to think: hang on, is this going anywhere? Generally, the customer, or fan, would disappear without having bought a book. Often they would say, 'I just love what you're doing here. It's great. Keep going! Bye!' And off they would go, with a warm feeling that they had been supportive.

But they had not spent a single penny. What was I doing? Running a free therapy centre? The other regular visitor would be the wealthy charity collector. Wives of bankers would come in and ask us to donate books to their charity for prisoners. The prisoners of London must be one of the most well-looked-after groups of rascals in the world. Rich wives are constantly teaching them how to read, write and create beautiful tapestry cushions.

'What's the point?' I would say, to anyone in earshot. I was exhausting myself, talking all day, often hosting an event until nine or ten, then drinking some beer to knock myself out. Thank God for the rest periods back home in Devon.

Finally, after five years, we closed our retail outlet. Our landlord, encouraged by the local estate agent, put the rent up by 30 per cent. So we decided the shop had done its job and that it was time to move on.

We have opted to follow the herd and sell online and at events rather than tying ourselves down to the relentless overhead of a retail rent. So, now, we 'pop up' everywhere, as the modern slang has it, selling our wares, telling people about the *Idler*, signing them up to subscriptions.

How to Sell

I am still learning a lot about selling. What I do know is that it's an art form and that it should be studied.

The first lesson is not to be *too* subtle about it. In the first few months after we opened the shop, people would come in and ask, 'Are the books for sale?' Of course, they're for sale! It's a bookshop!

But you can't blame customers for low sales. It's *your* fault. You have to make everything blindingly obvious, price-wise. Piles of books everywhere; lots of books facing outwards; that kind of thing. Our book sales in the shop improved when our manager, Julian Mash, started work at the *Idler*. Suddenly, the place looked more like a bookshop. Perhaps Victoria and I had been a little rash, thinking that we could run a bookshop, café and event space with no experience of doing any of them.

'Sales are hard things to get,' says Luke Johnson. Whether it's pizza, books, courses, coffee or bicycles, people do not part with their cash readily. You have to give them a good reason. You have to give them something they want, at the right price, and somehow make them think that they are being clever and have not been the victim of a hard sell. When I worked at a skateboarding shop, the bosses told us not to go in for the hard sell. It may work once, but that customer will never come back.

Here are a few very basic tips:

- You must genuinely like what you are selling. Time and again, we find that when we attempt to sell something because it seems to be hot at that point in time, it's very difficult. However, when we are excited about the thing (the book, event, magazine, tea towel, or whatever), it will fly.

- Build a website. This is your shop window and, in fact, your shop as well. It is possible to set one up for pretty much nothing. We'll go into more detail in the next chapter.

- Your website must include really good professional photos. We forked out £250 to get some decent photos done, and it was well worth it.

- Gather testimonials. We live in the age of reviews. Get some good customer feedback and tell everyone about it. Most people are sheep and will follow their friends and follow trends. Only a small percentage of the population are what is called 'early adopters' and will take risks.

- Try to get some professional or celebrity endorsement. If a figure with some sort of authority endorses what you are doing, it gives prospective buyers confidence in your company. When you have no money for marketing, having this back-up can work wonders. Murphy Williams, marshmallow entrepreneur, says that she made the mistake of paying for advertising on Facebook when she started out. It didn't work. 'But what did work was thinking of people in the public eye who might like the product, sending them some and then telling the world what their response was. Sophie Dahl tweeted that [the marshmallows] were sublime, which got picked up by the *Daily Mail*, which led to an avalanche of press, sales and now monthly new marshmallow start-ups. Her quote is still on my home page.'

- Put on events. Live events can provide cash, are enjoyable and a good way to meet your customers. Through events, you can gather email addresses. You can sell books or other products, have fun and make something happen which is really appreciated by the audience. Our whole business at the *Idler* is based on the old Greek idea of the symposium, a drinking party with wine at which serious and lightweight matters were discussed. The most famous one was attended by Socrates and is written up both by Plato and by Xenophon.

- Set up a stall at festivals. Festivals are great places to try out ideas. If, for example, you have an idea for a food business, then do *not*, under any circumstances, rent premises, unless you happen to be very well funded or own the freehold. Instead, go for a street-food business. Get your food out there. Some of these concerns make loads of money. I heard of one guy who sells crêpes from a van and makes two grand a day at the weekends, and he has practically no overheads. With street food, you are free.

- Set targets and KPIs. Yes, I know this sounds hopelessly unbohemian, but it works. KPIs are Key Performance Indicators, and could include sales figures, or newsletter sign-ups, Facebook reach or mentions in the press. You need to establish targets and goals, otherwise you will have no means of measuring your progress and will be like a piece of driftwood or a ball in a pinball machine, buffeted around by forces beyond your control. Of course, being bohemian, you should not get too depressed if you fail to meet the target.

Get the Right Product

This is easy to say, but try to make or sell something that people actually want, while keeping true to yourself. Like The Beatles, the ideal is to offer creations that are good *and* commercial. Stick to your guns. Everyone laughed when I commissioned and published a short book on old-school grammar from Latin teacher Mr Gwynne. What planet is he on? they thought. So eccentric. But, later, Random House approached me and published a commercial edition. They sold fifty thousand copies and the book was in the top ten for eight months.

So, you need to be bold. You also need to try lots of things and be stoic when some of them fail. You can't really know why some things work and some things don't.

I suppose a good rule to bear in mind is: would *you* buy this? If not, you are being dishonest or disingenuous. When cut-price jeweller Gerald Ratner said he was selling 'crap', it destroyed consumer confidence in his business. You should think like William Morris and only sell things that are beautiful and useful, or one of the two. Selling shoddy in a cynical way is simply wrong.

As Charlie Gladstone of Pedlars says, 'Only work with products and people you truly believe in.' Don't try something out because you are second-guessing your market or because you have seen a similar business do it.

An example: the writers of best-sellers do not think that they're writing rubbish. They think they're writing fantastic, fun books. They do not produce a commercial book cynically; commercial books are what they love to write. The best businesses really believe that they are doing something helpful for the customer, perhaps solving a problem for them, or creating something of great beauty. At the *Idler*, everything we do must be beautiful or useful, or both.

It's generally easy to sell something that you really like. But this rule does not always work. Right now, we are struggling to sell tickets to our medieval supper club. I am amazed. I thought that they would fly out.

Create a Club That People Want to Join

We have a lot of fun at the *Idler* and people want to join in. This, I think, is why our two best-selling products are our memberships and our magazine subscriptions. Our customers, readers and fans enjoy being part of a movement. I mentioned subscription-model businesses in Chapter 2 – think about how you can create a following for what you do and make people want to buy into your business model as a whole.

Do Not Oversell

When I send out my weekly or twice-weekly newsletters, I always worry that I will get a load of abuse back. Every so often, I get a complaint from a reader who says that I used to have something interesting to say but that I have, sadly, become a grubby pursuer of money and profits. My first response is to get angry and send them my accounts to prove that I earn about the same as a first-year trainee nurse.

But then I realize that it is just because I am not presenting myself very well. Maybe my attempts to sell are just too obvious. Maybe real salespeople don't make you feel like they are selling to you. Maybe you have to be subtle about it. This is the subject that used to be known as rhetoric, in other words, the art of persuasion, whether by words, speech or images, or a combination of these. There is an enormous amount of literature on the subject. And a lot of it is immoral, frankly. Selling can be scamming. But some of it is still worth a look, as it could help you to sell the good stuff you are doing or making.

When you start out, you think: we are not going to do discounts or offers or tawdry things like that. Our typesetter, Christian, has a phrase for vulgar overselling: 'I think you're getting too "Buy Daz!"' He makes the point that we are not selling soap powder. (Sometimes, I wish we *were* selling soap powder. I bet the margins are fantastic.)

But soon you will find yourself doing the odd sale and offering discount coupons.

Offer Bargains

We do offers every now and then. Some bohemians would advise you never to discount because cutting prices can devalue your brand. But I see nothing wrong with holding a three-day sale if you want to clear some stock or raise some cash. Last week, we did a sale on our *Idler* hardback annuals and raised nearly two grand in cash in three days. This was a great success and got us out of a hole, as our rent was coming up.

When we launch an online course, we often send a discount code to our newsletter subscribers. Sometimes, these work really well and we sell fifty to a hundred courses in one go, which just about covers the cost of production.

People do like bargains. Just don't do them too often, or your customers may not buy anything unless it's on sale. We often put a time limit on the bargain: this offer will expire in forty-eight hours – so get your skates on, madam!

Test It

Order a small amount of a particular product and test it out. We have just published a book, *The Idler Guide to Ancient Philosophy*. Our first run was a mere hundred copies, which cost us less than £200. That edition sold out in a few days, so we decided to do a bigger print run of 250 for the second edition. Try a small run at a high price to gauge demand.

The technical term for this process is 'Minimum Viable Product'. In Silicon Valley, they say: 'Ship something!' Just get going. When we launched our online courses, we recorded one to test the waters. That sold well, so we produced a second. Then we got investment and produced a further fourteen, all of which have sold pretty well. Now we plan to record a hundred brilliant courses with top teachers.

Offer Samples

Somehow or other, you need to get your product sampled. We recently sold fifty bottles of a friend's honey whisky at a stall at an art market for a tenner each. It was easy: we just gave people samples with a plastic spoon. They loved it and most of them immediately bought a bottle. It was like being one of those snake-oil salesmen in the westerns.

With our online courses, we produce a trailer, a little taster. Could you make videos of your products, offer a taste of the cake before selling the whole thing? Show spreads of the book? Include reviews? Look at what Amazon are doing. They employ the world's top brains, but you can look at their techniques right there on their website.

Bohemians often are excellent salespeople. This is because they believe in what they are doing. And whether you are editor of new-agey *Resurgence* magazine Satish Kumar, or Damien Hirst, or hedge funder Crispin Odey or the headmaster of Eton, your job is the same: asking other people for money so that you can continue to do what you do. Enjoy it.

Arguably, your most important sales tool is your website; it's your shop window and often the first port of call for a prospective customer. So now we're going to look at how to get yours set up.

8. The Importance of the Website

Il faut cultiver notre jardin.

— Voltaire, *Candide*

When we run our real-life Business for Bohemians course at the Idler Academy, our students complain that they lack knowledge in two main areas. The first is the money side: the accounting, the spreadsheets; the second is technology and their website. It's easy to feel overwhelmed by technology. Your website never seems quite good enough. Our students say that they feel at sea because they don't understand the basics. This makes them easy prey for geeks who blind you with science and charge you £700 a day.

Well, you don't need me to tell you that your website is of primary importance. As I said, it's your shop window and everyone expects you to have one, so every entrepreneur or bohemian businessperson would do well to get to grips with at least the rudiments of the technical ability required. I often hear people say, 'I'm no good at tech,' but it seems to me that a basic understanding of the tech is absolutely necessary for a bohemian business-owner these days.

Most small businesses experience website paranoia, the

creeping feeling I mention above that their site is not good enough. We worry that it is not updated often enough, it is not sufficiently connected to social media, it doesn't work properly, and so on. That is normal.

But you do need to learn the basics. Otherwise, you will spend a lot of money and wander around in a cloud of ignorance. 'Competence is at the root of happiness,' as the great William Cobbett once wrote.

Our Website Story

Like most businesses, we at the *Idler* started off spending £0 on our website. This is easier than you might think. I asked my friend Murphy, the one who started her own luxury marshmallows business, how much she spent on her very handsome website.

'Nothing! But I pay a commission on each sale to the ecommerce platform Shopify. They provide templates, apps, very helpful blogs and twenty-four-hour phone assistance or live chat, which was a blessing during the four solid days it took me to make the site, having never done one before. I can even do a bit of HTML now.'

Since we launched the *Idler*, we have gradually spent more money on our website as the years have gone by. In the noughties, I paid a friend £500 to create a nice-looking blog-based website. A year after launching the Idler Academy, we forked out £7,000 to a designer to create something more beautiful and professional which could handle the delivery of our online courses.

Later, we attracted investment so we looked for a new website company which could handle our e-commerce. We interviewed two possible companies, went with one of them, and spent £20,000 on a new website. The new site, built by young men with beards, had an instant effect. Overnight, we went from having fifty visitors a day to having five hundred. Now, we often get a thousand to two thousand people visiting our site each day. And we often take £1,000 a day or more via the site. Which is good.

Our website was created using WordPress, which is a simple CMS, or Content Management System. (Business is full of silly abbreviations, so I have supplied a glossary at the back of the book. I call them TLAs – Three-Letter Acronyms. A geeky one I like is UTS, used when a non-techie customer complains that the website doesn't work. It stands for 'User Too Stupid'.)

Our website is set up so that any of us on the *Idler* 'team' can create a new product, put up a video clip, blog post, long essay, podcast, article, online course – pretty much anything. There are those 'share' buttons at the foot of each article, so that readers can send the link to the piece out to their Facebook friends or Twitter followers. I don't like sending our hard-earned customers to those rival websites for free, but it seems this is compulsory these days.

I think it's actually quite wonderful that we can all run our own multimedia websites for a small amount of money. It's fun posting articles, pictures, podcasts. I love finding images from old medieval paintings: they look great on a computer screen.

What is less clear is how all the work we put into the website will translate into sales. For about a year, I spent hours every day updating our website with articles, pictures and video clips. We got a fair amount of traffic. But visitors are not the same as customers, so your website needs to lead these visitors to a place where they become customers.

That means sampling. Small pieces of cake. Your website should be a place where readers can buy what you do as easily as possible and which offers tasters of what you do. That's why I think it is wise to offer short video and sound clips on your website. Or a cheap 'Try out what we do' offer.

You get back what you put in: the more care you put into your little garden, the more people will enjoy it. That doesn't mean huge piles of work: it means wandering around it every day, watering, tending, deadheading, sowing and planting. You want a website that is low maintenance, that you can look after for yourself, like a garden.

Of course, there will be some technical issues that are beyond you. And this is when you need the kid. Right now, we are in the process of talking to various kids who will be able to come into the office and do a day here and a day there working on our website issues. The technology is great when it works but infuriating when it goes wrong. And it is very likely to go wrong. We have had whole weeks when we've had problems with our video clips. I had failed to realize that our video-hosting company was changing its business model: it suddenly started plastering our videos with ads for KFC, to the righteous horror and indignation of our customers. This meant that we had to find a new video-hosting company very quickly. We went with one called Sprout, which seems pretty good.

As the business owner, you will be bombarded with emails from staff, customers, friends and parents when something goes wrong. So it pays to have a modicum of understanding of the processes yourself and to make time to teach the others in your gang how to use it. They may well not pick it up by osmosis.

I suppose the most important thing when it comes to your website is to keep it looking fresh and up-to-date. Spending ten minutes a day updating it, introducing a new offer, posting a video clip or a picture is well worth it.

As with the spreadsheet and accounting, you need to learn how to love your website and not resent the extra toil it involves. And it is easy to get into that resentful state. Many are the times that I have ranted to Victoria at home, 'What's the point? I'm just spending time every day providing free entertainment!' Or I have said, 'I used to be a writer. Now I just drive traffic to my website. *What happened?*'

Your website is important because it is both a piece of branding and a shop. It may often be the first port of call for a customer, so you need to put yourself in their shoes. They have never heard of you – what is this thing, exactly? Never start your blog posts with the word 'I', because no one knows who you are. I notice when I'm on Google Analytics (of which more in a moment – this is import-ant) that people click on the 'about' link very often indeed.

So I worry about that page. Is it clear enough? Does it tell an engaging story?

My advice would be to keep the website natural and chatty and as simple as possible. When you're working out how the thing will look, study websites you like. We really loved the *New Yorker*'s simple, clean design, and so we tried to emulate that. We also wanted a classic English vibe. We liked the black-and-red of the *Spectator*. So that is the brief we gave the designer when we launched our twenty-grand website.

First Steps in Website Creation

It is likely that, at the beginning, you'll be creating a website with no money. To get your hand in, if you are making things, you might like to set up a page with a platform such as Etsy. This will give you a bit of free training. Then look at a service like Squarespace or Shopify. They take a monthly fee in return for helping you to pursue your dream.

(Which makes me think: there is more money in helping others to pursue a dream than in pursuing the dream itself. Etsy, all crowdfunding sites, website services, payment-gateway systems, Patreon (a 'help your favourite artist' platform), Coursera (where you can take short online courses offered by universities) – even eBay and Amazon – promote their services as a kind of route to freedom and money. But most of the sellers who take this route will be disappointed. They will not make a living.)

If you decide to graduate from the world of the free website, then you will need to find a designer. Big companies use expensive Soho agencies to create websites, looks, logos and branding devices for them. As a bohemian, you cannot afford them. You have £0, so you will have to be very resourceful.

You will have to look around your immediate acquaintances. Perhaps there is a young designer whose work you like and who will work for a modest fee, or for some sort of recognition and credit. And copy – or at least study – the big guys. If you look at the really big websites – Uber, Airbnb, Facebook – they are very simple indeed. So copy them. They have spent millions on the most advanced consumer research known to man. I have heard that Airbnb tries to create the same kind of feeling of safety you might feel in the womb, and they call this 'foetal marketing'.

They make everything BLINDINGLY OBVIOUS and print everything in HUGE TYPE so there is no ambiguity. Uber uses very few words to get its message across: 'Your ride, on demand'.

And most importantly, these companies are confident, and you must be confident yourself. The websites of Airbnb and Uber don't make you feel like you are renting out your spare room or driving a minicab – both of which used to be signs of having fallen on hard times. They make you feel like you are a part of an international jet set of independent and glamorous people, all of whom are totally in control of their aspirational, groovy lives.

You'll also notice the importance of imagery. The big sites spend fortunes on photography. And this is something you might be able to copy, on a budget. Do not use terrible snaps you have taken with your iPhone on your website. Employ a proper photographer, someone who understands composition, light, lenses. We used a friend named Dirk Lindner, a brilliant architectural and portrait photographer. His pictures have been worth their weight in gold and I do not regret for a second paying for them. The first batch took him a morning to do, cost us £250, and we are still using them five years later. Not only do they make our website look beautiful, we also have good-quality pictures to send to magazines and other press. This is good because the better the picture, the more space you are likely to be given. It would be wise to include a press pack on your website which includes hi-res pictures. This is something I still have to get round to. Do as I say, not as I do.

Remember, by the way, the power of barter. The above-mentioned Dirk, my photographer friend, will quite often come and photograph one of our events in return for a couple of free tickets. He's happy, we're happy.

Avoid being Seduced by the Latest Thing

There is always some fad that everyone tells you to get in on. Right now, it appears to be video. We met a Facebook bigwig, and he told us to make videos. That was the way to get more 'like's. That's obviously nonsense. A good video may well get 'like's but a bad one will not. The most shared post recently on our Facebook page was not a video but a long article I wrote about walking around London.

Keep doing what you want to do and don't get distracted by what is known as the 'shiny stuff'. You may end up spreading yourself too thin. In the case of the *Idler*, it was a breakthrough moment when we decided to start publishing a physical magazine again. Somehow, we had lost sight of our core product – an independent magazine – in our rush to keep up with the latest thing, and spent too much time providing free content – blogging, making videos and doing other stuff that simply does not make money.

Rather than filming our events, we've decided to make good-quality podcasts of them. It's far better to make a decent sound recording with the writer or celebrity in question and release this as a podcast on your website than to fork out on video. It's less work and you only have to bear the cost of the original recorder. (Buy one with two built-in mics and proper inputs so you can record direct from a mixing desk.) And listening to podcasts, I think, is a very *Idler*ish thing to do. Just lovely. The idea that you can be your own TV channel, while appealing, is a little unrealistic if you are turning over just £250,000, like us. Get to a million, and we'll take another look.

Embrace sound! Yes to radio! Yes to the wireless!

In the early days, don't get ideas above your station. I remember, many years ago, proudly showing John Brown an issue of the *Idler*. We had forked out on printing gold on the cover. This was called an 'extra colour' and involved a lot of extra cost. John Brown took a look and said without a moment's hesitation, 'You can't afford gold.'

He was right; it was a stupid decision and I doubt whether it led to one extra sale. Live within your means.

Running Your Website

On returning to London and relaunching the *Idler*'s website – with a new design and a self-made mandate to update it every day – I went to see my old friend James Brown (not John Brown). James was launch editor of now defunct lads' magazine *Loaded* and went on to become editor of GQ and to launch his own magazine company, IFG, which he sold to magazine tycoon Felix Dennis for over £6 million. He now runs a web-only magazine called *Sabotage Times* and is a real force of nature – a genius. 'Buy me lunch and I'll show you how it works,' he said.

So over lunch at a Japanese place of his choice in Charlotte Street in the West End, James sat me down and explained how we should get traffic moving. First, he said, I should get myself set up with Google Analytics: 'It's great. I have it open all the time, I feel like a City trader or something.'

Google Analytics shows how many people are on your website in real time. It tells you which country they are from, and how long they spend on the site. You can see when people are at the checkout and when they have put something in their basket. You can monitor the success of a Tweet on visitor numbers. You can also see how people got to your site and watch the effect of articles, mail-outs and publicity. When, for example, we ran a Q&A with the brilliant TV journalist Louis Theroux, our visitor numbers went up to eight thousand in a day from the usual five hundred.

'Don't worry about the home page!' James also said. 'They're out!'

This is because most people come to your website from a link to a specific article, so they will not necessarily even see the home page. I also discovered that James makes proper money from creating magazine sections for other websites and big companies. His own site, based on a free-content-with-ad-sales model, was tough going. At most, he said, he was only getting a few thousand pounds a month from ad sales, and now, he said, 'They've fallen off a cliff.'

I shelled out what seemed to me an enormous sum for our light bento lunch and went home. I immediately got us set up with Google Analytics and now, when working on the *Idler* site, I do as James advised and keep it open, like some sort of futures trader. Idleness in real time! Yeah, baby, hit me!

The Google Analytics page tells you how many unique users you are getting each week or month. At the time of writing, we have had 160,000 visitors in ten months, an average of around 16,000 a month. Sometimes, though, the results disappoint. I often look at the site and see that there is only one visitor on it, from the London area. Then I realize that I am that visitor.

The problem with websites is, I think, that they are so hungry for content. You have to feed them incessantly. But my message in this chapter is: study the digital world. Attempt to understand it. The website is your shop window and it can be fun, but be wary of spending too much time and money on the latest thing. A website brings freedom. To create one and maintain it is a creative act. Like a garden. So think long on it, and ponder.

So, now, you've got a website. Everyone around you starts asking, 'What is your social-media strategy? What about Twitter and Facebook?' In the next chapter, we're going to investigate the trials and tribulations of social media. Above all, you need to remember that social media is a business; its goal is to sell advertising. And as I advised you to do above, they aim to give you a free sample of what they can do in the hope that you will graduate to being a paying customer. So be careful.

9. The Disappointments of Social Media and How to Get It Right

Folly is wont to have more followers and comrades than discretion.

— Cervantes, *Don Quixote*

For the last ten years or so, small business owners have been subjected to relentless commercial and cultural pressure to use social media to promote their enterprise. Every tiny village pub seems to be on Twitter. You can even pay to go on courses which tell you how to use these social-media websites. Companies employ social-media people and boast, 'This is the amazing Clara, who does our social media.'

The social-media platforms themselves — Facebook, Twitter and the rest — profit from selling ad space or being paid to promote your brand, or your club, to your friends and followers in a more assiduous manner than it has been sold or promoted before.

The question is: what is the proper bohemian response to this? And also, does all this Tweeting and Facebooking actually work, from a commercial perspective?

Let me make this much clear: I've never really liked Facebook. It seems to me like an ad-sales scam combined with a data-gathering exercise: a very cynical operation.

The obvious point to make about it is: it is a means of selling ad space. In return for using its service, users like you and me allow ourselves to be sold to the companies which buy ad space on Facebook. With Facebook, you are not the customer, you are the product. An early ad line they used was: 'We want everyone to use Facebook.' The company's growth strategy was based on the philosophical idea that people are sheep. And it worked.

At times, I have become increasingly exercised about this issue. I remember having a chat with my friend Matt Stinchcomb, who is high up at the online sell-your-wares company Etsy. We hatched a plan to create something called The Anti-Social Network. We'd have our own logo, and individuals and companies would join us. We would defend the right to be grumpy, negative and cynical. Because that's another of my objections to social media: the relentless, grinding positivity. Everyone on Twitter seems to be in a constant state of excitement. 'Excited to be releasing our new app! So excited to be meeting with blah blah! Excited to be eating a lonely sandwich in a park on my lunch break.'

Well, maybe Matt and I should have had the courage of our convictions. Maybe we should have gone anti-social. I have just read about an app called Cloak which was launched by Chris Baker, a founder of the news website Buzzfeed (whatever that may be). Cloak blocks people from your life and gives you privacy. Says Baker, 'I think that the age of mass social networking has reached its peak. Platforms like Facebook and Twitter are public arenas where we cultivate versions of ourselves that are well manicured, mostly false, and always "on". I think that is what's beginning to wane. We're exhausted from it and by it. Now platforms that enable ephemeral, private and very loose moments are starting to become hugely mainstream. Anti-social stuff is on the rise. Social has had its moment in the sun. Now people are beginning to revolt.'

How Social Media Could Actually Damage Sales

Now this is a radical theory. I reckon that social media, far from increasing your sales, could actually damage them. Why? Because instead of buying your product, people just retweet a post from you. For example, someone may want to appear to their friends as the kind of person who likes the *Idler*. In the old days, they would have had to buy a book or a magazine or a ticket to an event.

With social media, I merely have to 'like' or 'retweet' and the job is done. If someone 'like's the *Idler* and broadcasts that fact to their friends, then their friends will see them as an *Idler*-type person without them having to put their credit-card details on the line. It's for this reason that I worry that marketing on Facebook has the potential to damage your business.

It's the same with Twitter. Instead of buying the product, for example, *The Idler Guide to Ancient Philosophy*, your followers just retweet a link to it that you just tweeted. This way, their friends think that they are the kind of brainy person who is interested in ancient philosophy.

Should You Therefore Reject Social Media?

In an ideal world, I would not use Twitter or Facebook. And if you are brave enough, it is not unfeasible to reject them altogether.

I think it's great that *Monocle* magazine, the business founded by publishing genius Tyler Brûlé, who before that founded *Wallpaper*, essentially rejects the seductions of social media. He says, 'I think many media brands will find, or are finding, it's a brilliant way of also diluting your brand.'

When you build a bohemian brand, you need to ask yourself whether all the effort and time spent on Facebook and Twitter could be better spent doing something else – something fun, something that gets you publicity. And since Twitter and Facebook make everything look the same, could it, as Tyler suggests, in fact damage your brand to be on them?

Keep asking yourself: what is the point of all this? To me, it is about harmonizing freedom, creativity and money-making into a satisfying whole. Your business is an umbrella for you to test out your ideas.

And yet, after much philosophical hand-wringing, I have come to accept that social media does have its benefits. While it might not be a particularly effective direct-sales channel, it can be a useful tool for building awareness. If used wisely, it does not cost anything and need not take up too much of your time. It is a means of communication, and business is all about telling people what you do. It is a form of community, and brands are all about community. People across the world love it. It makes them feel modern. And nearly two billion people can't be wrong, I suppose.

It can have practical applications, too. Customers use Facebook or Twitter to praise or complain, and they expect a prompt response. One week, we released a new book and had a terrific response: it sold out in three days. But we also had issues. Customers got stuck in our payment system. Some of them Tweeted about it – 'Your website is broken!' – and we were able to get straight back to them and sort out their order.

Just occasionally, there are major benefits. It's worth posting something on your page every day or two, as you just never know what is going to happen. Recently, I was sitting on a coach heading back into London following an Easter weekend away, dozing a little as we drove past Stonehenge. My phone rang. It was the *Evening Standard*, asking for my comment on the Facebook backlash.

I sat up. What Facebook backlash?

'Well, there are quite a few comments saying that £20 is too high a ticket price for an event about the gentrification of London.'

Ah yes. I had applied my 'keep the price high' philosophy to a debate on gentrification in London. I had seen one or two comments complaining about the price, and hastily introduced a 50 per cent reduction for concessions. But, it seems, I was too late. We were beset by students thinking they were witty by saying things like: 'A debate on this subject and they charge £20? What a joke.' After that, the London *Metro* called me, and then the

Independent. I was able to tell them all that there was a half-price concession and, in any case, that we are a small arts organization and we have to pay our staff and the speakers, and so on. And that we have no outside funding.

The result of all this publicity was that orders flooded in, we had a record week as far as website visitors goes and we had to move the event to a larger venue. So, thank you, Facebook. But that little viral happening was completely unplanned and unexpected.

And another thing: social media is fun. I enjoy sending pithy quotes from our articles on to Twitter. We have ten thousand followers, and perhaps five or ten might click on the link. Some of them may 'share' it with their friends and followers. So it's OK. I don't mind it. It probably won't lead to any sales, but it's quite fun. And it is probably best for the business owner to do it, at least when the business is small, because they, after all, will be the best person to communicate the personality of the business. Just don't get addicted.

I also enjoy putting a link up on our Facebook page every day or so. Put up the right piece of writing, a poem, a video or sound clip, and people will share it with each other. This means that they are telling their friends about your business, and some of those friends may become new customers.

It's enjoyable to see that our articles are being shared hundreds or thousands of times −far more than you get on the *Spectator,* or even the *Guardian,* in many cases. By the way, funny is good. People will share jokes. The first time we featured this cartoon from the geniuses Modern

Toss on our website we had thousands of shares. So be funny and be natural.

The trick is learning how to be a master of social media and how to avoid allowing social media to be a master of you.

Don't Waste Money on It

Like any business, we at the *Idler* are always trying to recruit new customers. Like a band, we think what we do is great and we want to find fans. So we like to get the word out there by any means possible. Social media can obviously help with that mission, and the good thing about social media is that it is free.

But, like any business, Facebook is working hard to extract dollars out of you. They give you poor results for your 'reach', or whatever, and then tempt you into paying money to 'boost' your post. The bohemian must resist!

Do not spend money chasing 'like's and retweets. You would do far better to create an engaging piece of creative content — a poem, a story, an interview, an arresting image, a video — and recycle it on Twitter, Facebook and all the rest. And always use social media as a way of getting people to come back to your own website by including a link in your tweet or post.

The steps to follow are these: create a new article on your website; copy the link and paste it on to your Facebook page or Twitter feed; choose a picture and add a little comment. This ensures that people will click on your website to read the full article and move away from whichever social-media site you posted it on.

We also need to remember that there are traditional forms of communicating — like producing flyers and talking to people — which are just as effective as social media at spreading the word. One of the easiest and most effective forms of publicity, I think, is to organize events, happenings and parties. If a hundred people come to a party and have a great time, every one of them will tell another ten people. That is like retweeting — but real. We throw a party every quarter to launch the new issue of our magazine. We charge £10 and sell 150 tickets (the people who come get a free copy of the mag, too). This way, we make a few quid and have fun at the same time.

How about hosting a monthly DJ night at a bar? I have never regretted giving a party and, after all, that is genuinely social. Even better, you don't have to give the ad-sales guys at Facebook or Twitter a penny.

Awards and competitions are excellent schemes, too. When we were discussing promoting our book *Gwynne's Grammar* with Random House, I suggested that we launch something called the Bad Grammar Award. 'Great idea,' said Jake Lingwood, the publisher. 'Do it!' So we did it, and it has turned into an annual media event. It's been covered in all the national newspapers and the *Hindustan Times*. We got proper national PR coverage: far superior to a million tweets.

People love taking sides in the grammar debate, and it has been enormous fun. Yes, we get attacked, but we get praise as well. This was a far better trick than paying some millennial to tweet for us.

You will need to get out there. Far better than sitting at home tweeting is to go out to launches, gigs, theatres, cafés, pubs and festivals and just wander about a lot. Organize events at festivals, hand out flyers and go for very long walks.

When it comes to selling what you make, which is the ultimate goal of business, you might also think about using the old telephone. At this moment, we are calling round and emailing a load of bookshops to ask whether they will stock the *Idler*. We spent ten minutes on this, with the result that five branches of Waterstones have agreed to stock the magazine.

Don't Waste Too Much Time on It

Now here is an issue that I am starting to get my head around. I have noticed that if I sit at my laptop and tweet all day long, then we may make one or two extra sales. But there are days when I cannot sit there tweeting all day because I have gone on a six-day silent retreat. Or I'm hungover.

So you need to schedule your tweets and your blog posts. For some reason, I seem to find this kind of fore-sight impossible, so I sit down with Julian, *Idler* deputy editor, who is far better organized than I am. You can sit down for an hour with a program like TweetDeck and plan your tweeting. Do ten a day – that doesn't take too long. As James Brown said, 95 per cent of your followers will not have seen the previous tweet. And if you are try-ing to talk to a global audience, you could schedule them to ping into the ether in the middle of the night.

Scheduling means making more effort at the begin-ning, but it will also mean that you can spend a weekend doing nothing without worrying, confident in the knowl-edge that your tweets are being sent and new pieces are being posted on your website.

Good business management is not about hard work. Hard work, in the sense of very long hours, is for stupid people, or disorganized ones, or fearful ones. Careful thought and planning, and the creation of good systems, can lead to plenty of free time and plenty of sleep for you. And you'll avoid the overwork which can lead to a breakdown.

Don't Expect Too Much from It

If you think that you can send a few tweets and put a post on Facebook and just sit back and watch the sales come flooding in, you will be sorely disappointed. Social media alone does not a marketing strategy make.

The other point about Twitter is that there is a huge difference between having a million followers and having 263, which is about how many publicity departments have. Often you get retweeted and you think, Ah, how nice. Then you click on the person's profile and find they have 123 followers, none of whom will see the tweet.

And even millions of followers may not be great for sales. The great Twitter victim and liberal icon Stephen Fry once retweeted a link to an event we were running with the producers of the TV show *QI*, which Fry used to present. This was accompanied by much hoo-ha from his 'people' about what to do when Lord Fry deigns to favour you with a retweet. 'Be careful,' they said. 'The extra traffic could destroy your website. You should contact your server administrator.'

What poppycock. Fry retweeted to his five million – whatever – followers, and we sold eight tickets for the event and picked up a hundred new followers. OK, I'm not complaining. Far from it. Thank you, Stephen. I am just making the point that Twitter is hugely over-rated as a promotional tool. Vanity, all vanity.

What profiteth a man if he hath ten million Twitter followers but oweth his money-lender fifty crowns? Vanity, sheer vanity!

One more thing: I object to the phrase 'tipping point', invented by author Malcolm Gladwell. I have never seen this tipping point, where suddenly, overnight, your business goes crazy, either within my own business or that of anyone else I know. The reality is that things will take a long, long time, much longer than you think, even in your worst estimates. Growth is slow, very slow. I raised this point during a seminar with Luke Johnson. He said, 'How many small businesses has Malcolm Gladwell run?'

Things, basically, don't go viral. Things don't just 'take off'. You may be the lucky recipient of a stroke of luck in the wider world – a change in legislation, in a tax law or a social trend. But in the main, business is about process and small steps. One tiny step at a time. As I mentioned in the introduction to this book, you should probably allow yourself a business apprenticeship of seven years. That's how long it takes to become a reasonably good carpenter. Why should it be any quicker to become a reasonably good businessman?

Use It Wisely and Well

So, if you are going to use social media, use it well. Avoid spending money on it if you run a small business. Remember that time spent on it is time lost elsewhere. And remember that it is not a substitute for genuine engagement with customers.

As a bohemian in business, you are trying to communicate something, and you are trying to get fans for what you do. So you should always remember to do what you want. Be like David Bowie, who said that things went wrong for him when he started making work in order to please an audience rather than himself.

10. The Power of the Mailing List

He wins every hand who mingles profit with pleasure, by
delighting and instructing the reader at the same time.

– Horace

We saw in the previous chapter how spending money on digital-marketing efforts through social media can be a waste of time. The worst £2,000 we ever spent was on a silly Search-Engine-Optimization effort, or SEO, as the geeks like to say. We spent something like £500 of that on Google AdWords and could trace not one single sale to any one of them.

That £2,000, I reflected, would have been better spent on content. We could have paid Helen Fielding to write us a short story. It would have been wonderful to have commissioned some creative work with the money instead of forking out on some dodgy digital campaign which no one saw, and passing on even more money to the geeks.

Yes . . . unless you are very careful, the geeks, accountants and landlords will be the only ones to profit from your attempts to make your business dreams come true. Very sadly, like everyone else, I seem happy to spend £700 a day to hire a geek to set up a website and advise me to throw money at Google AdWords, while spending very little on the creative side – the content. Creatives – writers, photographers, artists – are asked to work for nothing while the geeks rake in piles of cash. That is going to change, I hope: I see signs that the creative economy will re-emerge as the tech companies start to rediscover their inner poet.

The best marketing, in our experience, is word of mouth, national press, real advertising (when you can afford it) and, best of all, email marketing. Expand your mailing list. All the time. For ever.

Sending warm, chatty emails to your customers keeps you in touch with them. It opens the channels of communication. It is like talking and selling stuff at a market stall. It gets your views and values across. It can entertain. And it leads to people spending money on the stuff that you do: every time I send an email to our list, I see a spike in sales.

Sending an email to your subscriber list is a lot harder to do than bunging something on Facebook or banging out a Tweet in the forlorn, desperate hope that it will go viral. But it works. It is by far our best way of generating actual sales rather than just good vibes, which, as soon becomes apparent, do not pay the rent.

But you will have to learn how to increase the size of your mailing list, and there are ways of doing this. We spend a lot of time running competitions and doing swaps with other magazines and like-minded companies: we send our people to them, and they send their people to us.

Our Newsletter Story

I have been building up a list of newsletter subscribers for many years. When we had set a date to open the Idler Academy, in March 2011, I was able to spend the previous three months selling courses and event tickets to our existing subscriber base, which was around four thousand at the time.

It worked. We sold a few thousand pounds' worth of tickets for both events and courses before we opened, directly from the mailing list.

We used a company called YMLP and paid them something like £100 per month. We now use a more up-to-date service called MailChimp. (MailChimp, TaskRabbit, SurveyMonkey – I am thinking of doing a new start-up called WorkSnail for people who want to avoid full-time employment.) Using YMLP was horrific. I would lose hours of work because the site was so user-unfriendly that you could easily press the wrong button and would have to write the whole thing again. Each week, I suffered real pain for three or four hours.

MailChimp is far easier to use, and now I enjoy writing the newsletters: I try to keep them amusing and opinionated. To me, they are freedom. I can do what I like. I can attack Google and Uber and celebrate the printed word.

We use the font Courier New, the typewriter one, because it looks immediate and old-fashioned, like a communiqué sent by Comandante Marcos of the Mexican Zapatistas. The newsletters are a great way to communicate with customers, fans and readers. People feel involved in what we are doing.

At parties, people say to me, 'I love your newsletters – they are the only ones I don't delete!' This is because they are not bland and inoffensive. They are ranty, and often negative. One week I ranted about the evil monopoly Uber. (My friend Rebecca Harris, a Tory MP recently voted fifth-sexiest member of the House of Commons, wrote back, saying, 'Are you running a business or an anti-Tory blog?')

You need to grow a thick skin, though, if you put provocations out into the ether. Readers are very happy to abuse me. Sometimes, for example, people on the left are offended by my newsletters. One week there was a story in the papers that a Tory MP had been caught playing Candy Crush on his phone during a meeting on pension reform. I thought this showed a sweetly human side and suggested that we enter him for our Idler of the Year competition.

The socialist readers of the *Idler* raged. In certain circles, you are not allowed ever to say anything positive about a Tory, ever. Tories are scum and, if you don't toe this Party line, you will be ejected by the Leninists. Some of these subscribers demanded to be unsubscribed. You have to let them go. If you want to write a lively newsletter, you have to be controversial, and if people take against it, they can choose not to read any more.

Anyway, back to the topic at hand . . .

How to Get People to Open Your Newsletters

We spend a lot of time thinking about our newsletter strategy, and MailChimp makes this process a little more scientific, with its precise measurements and reports. Here is an example of the sort of thing they provide:

For the bohemian of temperament, looking at your reports can make for painful viewing. Sensitive artists that we are, we tend to take it personally if we get a low 'open rate'. Or when people unsubscribe. MailChimp (ungrammatical slogan: 'Send Better Email') and the like fire numbers at you relentlessly. The numbers do not lie; they do not forgive. If only 15 per cent of those on your mailing list open your email, three hundred of those click and nobody buys a single thing that you are promoting, you are likely to get depressed.

There are loads of factors playing into this. What about your subject line – was it something that made people think they wanted to read the newsletter? The best open rate we ever had was for a newsletter called 'Bees and Poetry'. Why, I have no idea. Maybe the simplest explanation is the right one: our audience loves the idea of keeping bees and of reading poetry.

You can become obsessed with your open rates, to the extent that you start to make an effort to think like that dreadful magazine *Vice* (the *Daily Mail* for children) or the *Daily Mail* (*Vice* for adults), and try to produce something shocking, like: 'A British man is going to prison for having fish porn on his home computer.'

Here are a few of our newsletter titles, along with the percentage of opens they received:

Forget Mindfulness; Embrace Mindlessness. Plus, Will Self and Andrew Keen Ask: 'Has the Internet Ruined Everything?'
22.5 per cent

Learn the Secrets of the Ancients with Our New Guide to Ancient Philosophy
18.2 per cent

Sale: 50 per cent off the *Idler* this Weekend + Idling for Women
15.4 per cent

Medieval Italian Supper, Scottish Dancing and The Internet is Not the Answer
28.7 per cent

The lesson here, I think, is: lead with the idea. Your

customers will buy into an attitude and a philosophy first, and buy later. I think they also like hearing your honest reports about the ups and downs of your business and your daily life.

We find it tricky to keep the sales up *and* to keep our old-school anti-capitalist idlers happy. I guess that's my fault for starting an anti-consumerist business. Occasionally a subscriber will complain that we are sending out too many newsletters and being too crassly commercial and not idle enough. But if we decrease the rate, then our sales slump. And no one writes in to say, 'Thank you for not sending me an email for the last ten days.'

So, sadly, we have to risk annoying one in 22,000 people. I mean, Coca-Cola and Google don't worry about annoying people with excessive advertising. Apple doesn't say to itself, I think people have heard enough from us lately. Let's take a break.

The time of day that you send these newsletters is supposed to have an impact. I hear that the recruitment company reed.co.uk sees a spike in opens at lunchtime on a Monday, because that's the time when depressed office workers dream of finding a better job. We reckon that, for us, Tuesday at noon is a good time, but that's really only an impression we have. I suppose big companies have whole departments working on this stuff. As a small business, you will have to do it on your own.

You could drive yourself mad trying to work out when best to send out your newsletters. But if you are honest and generous, then they will be read and shared whenever you send them.

Newsletter Segmentation

Not long ago we went along to a warehouse space in East London for a meeting with the *Guardian* newspaper about their planned new event space in King's Cross. Various partners had been invited to give a talk about their plans for live events. In my view, the event was a tad pretentious. As I gave my presentation, an illustrator sketched live interpretations of the talk on a giant piece of paper.

Anyway, it was the first time I heard the phrase 'audience segmentation archetypes', but it was a phrase that I very much enjoyed trotting out whenever I could in subsequent meetings. Audience segmentation means breaking your list of customers into different groups: event-lovers, Londoners, high-spenders, over-fifties, under-thirties, or whatever. It's an important thing to do because, if you don't do it, then you may waste a lot of energy emailing someone who is never going to be interested in a particular product you are selling. Ask a young person to help you with this process. Alternatively, MailChimp and the other mailing-list programs offer online tutorials on this sort of thing and, if you can find the time, I would look into it.

How you get information about the demographics of your audience is another issue. An online questionnaire we sent out was quite successful. A company that was sponsoring some of our events wanted some information on who our customers were, so we mailed out a form and offered a prize of £100 to the entry that was drawn out of a hat. We got six hundred replies, which wasn't bad. And then we produced a report which gave us some great information: for example, that half of our customers are self-employed.

By the way, the *Guardian* dumped its events-hub idea. The project collapsed a year later when they realized that they didn't have £25 million spare to build an events venue but were in fact losing £50 million a year. This is because the advertising revenue from their free website disappeared when advertisers decided to spend their money on Facebook and Google instead.

Increasing Numbers on Your Mailing List

Our constant aim is to increase the size of our mailing list. Just as a band wants more fans and a writer wants more readers, a business, naturally, wants to recruit new customers.

Like any other part of business, unfortunately, the only way to make your mailing list bigger is through constant effort and tedious toil. When it comes to the mailing list, as in so many other areas, there is no 'tipping point' and I curse the name of Gladwell for putting this corrosive idea out there.

How do we do this? In many ways. We sign people up at live events and ask people on our existing list to get their friends involved. We send coupon codes offering discounts to friends who have businesses with similar types of customer to us. We hand flyers out at festivals.

We also run Facebook and Twitter competitions which require the user to join our mailing list. (Yes, I know I said I don't like them, but other people inarguably do.) When we really started to think about how to add subscribers to our mailing list, we noted down different things to try on a Google Doc and met each week to run through it.

The best way to increase your mailing list is to ask your existing customers to sign up a friend. The story goes that Dropbox was struggling. They then decided to offer free cloud storage space to users who recommended them to friends and family. A month later, users had sent out 2.8 million invitations to join.

We now have 22,000 on our list, but what we'd really like is 220,000. Such is the tyranny of growing a business: you will never be happy with where you are.

Connection with Your Fans

Our newsletter is a means of communicating directly with our customers. And our customers contribute to our website with their witty letters and pictures: we run a column called 'Sleeping Dogs and Sleeping Cats', in which we publish amusing photos of dozing canines and felines. Our readers are very helpful in other ways: they tell us when things aren't working. And they send us interesting links. In fact, the readers give me more than I give them. The *Idler* is all about being part of a community who want to enjoy their lives and be independent, and the mailing list is the beating heart of that.

It's not just me who writes the newsletters. Victoria and Julian write them, too. There is always the possibility that I might die tomorrow, so we need to be able to keep things going without me. I suppose that is the reason companies develop a sort of weird, inhuman corporate voice, the voice that speaks in advertising and on flyers and so on. The company must live on, even after its founders die, even though the staff changes. Certainly, I would like to see the Idler Academy live on in some way into the future as an educational institution: after all, Plato's Academy survived for around nine hundred years.

A note of caution: when you connect with your fans and readers with your mailing list, you may also find that they expect a pretty quick reply from you if they drop you a line. My feeling is that you should make every effort to get straight back to them. We all know what it's like when we send an email and don't receive a reply for days. Did they get the email? Have I offended them? These are the thoughts that go through your mind. So try to reply swiftly to customers – or get your staff to.

Your relationship with your customers requires constant nurturing. And that goes for your suppliers and the people you do business with as well. In addition, though, you must be careful and ensure that you make deals that work for you; otherwise, you will wander around in a fog of regret and bitterness. The next chapter will show you how to negotiate that deal.

11. The Art of Negotiation

Weakness overcomes strength. Softness overcomes hardness.
— Lao Tzu

My own tendency when it comes to money is to be over-generous at first and then get angry later with both myself and the rest of the world when I realize that I've made a mistake in being so.

When I get money, I have an irresistible urge to share it out again without keeping any for myself. It's a character fault. This happened in the early days of the Idler Academy. We collected over £200,000 a year from the sales we got and redistributed it to a raggle-taggle band of brilliant writers, poets, actors, musicians, lawyers, accountants, staff, book-keepers and artists, after having paid the really important people, that is, the landlord, the bank, the council, HMRC and the utilities companies.

I got zero.

I also made the mistake of being over-generous when Victoria won us a deal to produce a book about electricity for Vauxhall Motors, who were launching a new electric car. The money they offered us was actually fairly reasonable. But I overspent and did not leave any over for myself. For example, I commissioned some great writers, including Will Self and historian Jenny Uglow, and paid each of them £2,000 for a 2,000-word article. This is a top rate.

We made a small profit of £100, which went back into the business to pay staff, rates and rent. But I had neglected to put in a fee for my own work. It is all too easy to undervalue yourself in this way as a bohemian in business.

I overpaid people who spoke or did demonstrations at our events as well. In the first year of the Idler Academy I declared that we were going to pay these people properly. Too long, I said, have writers been expected to give talks at literary festivals for nothing. They need to live! We would pay them £100 or even £200 to give a ninety-minute talk, which would include a question-and-answer session.

Several charming bohemian poets and writers we worked with complained that 1) the ticket price for their event was too high and 2) we were not paying them enough. 'No one's going to pay £20 to see me,' the talent would moan, and then, 'I'm not doing it for £100.' There was a lack of logic there, but they couldn't seem to see it.

I Learn a Lesson about Negotiation

I learned through all this that something was wrong with my approach to negotiation. Some lack of confidence on my part was not only leading me to do deals that didn't work for me but also making the talent think they were getting a bad deal as well. I was creating lose-lose situations.

We are a purely commercial organization, unlike other arts organizations, which both charge high prices on the door and enjoy generous funding from state bodies. But if I point that out, it makes me sound a bit shrill and defensive. So I've found a better solution: let Julian deal with it. He is better than me at doing the deals. Perhaps he is less emotional than me, and less attached to the outcome. When it comes to larger commercial deals – for example, setting a fee for organizing a load of events for a big company – I have another associate do them. He gets a cut. So I would advise bohemians to do the same if at all possible: bring in a third party, either a staff member or a consultant, to close your deals.

You have to be mean. I've noticed that the bigger the organization, often, the meaner it is. The BBC, for example, is just like every other mean weakling out there: it pays huge sums to a handful of top brass and talent, and nothing or tiny amounts to the toilers in the middle who do all the work. Selfridges negotiated very hard with us as well. Clearly, they have learned the hard way: an over-generous business will die. It seems that we small guys need to toughen up.

We often work with the Soho House group, putting on events for their members. If they think they can, the people who work there will try to get away without paying us a penny. 'We get people to give talks for nothing, and they bring their friends, who spend money,' a Soho House manager said to me once. Instead, they will offer us, say, a year's free membership. That sounds good, until you realize that you can't afford to buy food and drinks there because no one is paying you properly.

Bohemian Negotiators

La Salle des Conferences

The difficulty for bohemians when negotiating is that we tend to be sensitive souls. Maybe even too nice to be in business. As Charlie Gladstone says, 'I have had endless disasters and been ripped off by endless people because I am too nice to be truly good at business.'

Still, this process of being ripped off and making mistakes will toughen you up as the years go by. And, in any case, successful bohemians are often pretty ruthless – just as ruthless as the business leaders who will let no one and nothing stop them or stand in their way. Joe Strummer rejected his old hippie mates when he met the Sex Pistols and became a punk. Bands will often throw out an affable but useless member who is getting in the way of their ambition. Pete Best, formerly of The Beatles, springs to mind. And Noel Gallagher of Oasis had no qualms about sacking people.

Bohemians often conceal their tough, businesslike natures and pretend that success 'just happened' to them, whereas the reality – whether you are Patti Smith, or Bono, or Lars Ulrich of Metallica or Stuart Murdoch of Belle and Sebastian – is that successful artists are hugely ambitious. They work at it. They will do anything for it. The Beatles, clearly, were hugely ambitious, and competitive, to boot.

Artists sometimes have to make difficult decisions, as do entrepreneurs. Often, I'm afraid to say, their work will take precedence over anything else, including their family. Barbara Hepworth famously decided that her responsibility to her own talent took precedence over her responsibility to her children, and her triplets were cared for by others.

Over the years, many bad things will happen in your business. People will copy your ideas and steal them, they will try to destroy your business, they will ask you to do a ton of work while dangling a carrot in front of you then toss you aside without a by-your-leave. But the people who do such things are as likely to be bohemians as businesspeople. You only have to read a biography of a rock band or a writer to find that out. The path ahead is lined with danger.

You will have to learn to play hardball. But how can you do this without turning into a complete tosser? The answer is to have a fall-back, a Plan B. Line up a plan B that you are perfectly happy with. That means that the other party in Plan A will not pick up an off-putting whiff of desperation. For example, we are currently fund-raising. The funds, if we get them, will help us to employ more staff, produce more online courses and generally acceler- ate our growth. But if we fail, we are happy to continue in a smaller, slower way. That would be fine. So we genu- inely do not care if Plan A doesn't happen: that way lies strength. Plan B might be 'do nothing'. Let's say that I am asked to give a talk. I say, 'Yes, if you pay me £500.' If they say no, then I am happy, because I can stay in bed instead of doing the talk. Naomi Campbell, brilliantly, taught us that trick. Unless you pay me £x, then I'd rather stay in bed.

Also, you have to learn to approach each individual or business you work with differently. You need to put a bit of time in and find out what it is that they want out of the relationship. Is it money, fun, exposure, gratitude, meaning?

Avoid Negotiation Altogether

One way of negotiating is to delegate the process to some- one else. You could create a fictional 'money man' who works at your company. Then you can say this sort of thing: 'I would love to pay you more, but our money man would never allow it.' Blame this money man, even if he doesn't exist. In Evelyn Waugh's *Vile Bodies*, hero Adam, an author, is being offered a comically terrible deal by his publisher. The publisher proposes the deal to Paul and then says that he'll 'square it with old Rampole':

> It was fortunate, he reflected, that none of the authors ever came across the senior partner, that benign old gentleman, who once a week drove up to board meetings from the country, whose chief interest in business was confined to a little book of his own about bee-keeping, which they had published twenty years ago, and though he did not know it, allowed long ago to drop out of print.

I now use Julian to play this trick. For example, when I am contacted to give a talk, he will always ask for a fee of £1,000 whereas if I was doing the negotiating I would probably settle for £150. And Victoria would get cross.

I need for there to be a point where I can say, 'I don't deal with that stuff. Talk to Julian.' And, recently, our friend James Pembroke, publisher of *Oldie* magazine, has agreed to look at our accounts each month. So I might start saying, 'I'll have to square it with old Pembroke,' when discussing terms with authors.

Now, if someone is being very difficult it may be best to walk away and cut your losses. We once had a customer who complained one summer that he had not received all the goodies he'd been promised for signing up to our membership scheme. I apologized and gave him a refund. But he remained on the warpath and complained loudly about wobbly tables during the handwriting class. And gave Tarquin, who was working there at the time, a telling-off for being chaotic. So I decided to ban him. I wrote to him, this time refunded him for the remaining lessons on the course, and asked him not to visit the Academy again. We just didn't need that kind of headache. (I later realized that he was probably mentally ill and on medication, because the tone of his emails veered so sharply from furious to charming.)

I recently heard the story of a gym owner who found his liberation when he realized that he could ban customers. He said that 90 per cent of his customers were fantastic, while 10 per cent seemed to make a career of whingeing, complaining, moaning and generally making his life a misery. Nothing was ever good enough for them, whether they were offered refunds, discounts, adjustments, improvements or whatever following their complaint. After years of spending a disproportionate amount of time and money trying to keep these whingers happy, the owner suddenly decided that he'd rather not have their business and simply banned them all. His life improved overnight.

So do not be afraid to rid yourself of troublesome customers. One woman I banned threatened that she would start a local bad-mouthing campaign and slag us off to all the people in the area she knew. Whether she did this or not, I have no idea. We certainly saw no sign of it.

Expert Advice on Negotiating

As part of our Business for Bohemians course, I invited former corporate lawyer and now consultant Hilary Gallo to give a class. Hilary has spent years trying to work out how to be tough without being a tosser. He has developed an approach to negotiation he calls 'the power of soft'. He rejects what he calls the 'tanks on the lawn' approach and focuses instead on trying to discover common ground between the two parties.

The basis of Hilary's approach is how to get what you want without being a complete bastard. So it suits the bohemian mindset well.

Any negotiation you enter into should not be a battle between a loser and a winner. You should aim to create a win-win situation. To do this, you need to be clear on what you want, and also to discover what the other party wants to get out of the project. You can start by pondering what it is that you want out of your life and your business. Money? Fun? Publicity? You may want a well-paid job which will help your cash flow. You could be open about this from the start. And what about the business you are negotiating with? What do they want? You may find that, if you're dealing with a big company, they want your creativity and input, to make them look groovy. They might want an ego boost, for you to summon up a room full of adoring fans. They might want to do something interesting because they are bored, or to do something 'good'. Or they might just want to make some money out of the deal.

You need to listen very carefully to what you are saying in the negotiations, and listen very carefully indeed to the other person. You should not need to use threats, as a certain editor of the *Sunday Times* did in the eighties. If an executive questioned a decision or command that Neil had made, the tough Scot would simply say: 'How big is your mortgage?' The executive would then mumble and go quiet. You need to be prepared to walk away.

I asked Hilary to offer a few tips from his long experience and all the reflection he's done on the subject. He addressed the issue of bohemianism. In a nutshell, he says that bohemians often have big ideas about their own talents but, weirdly, undervalue themselves at the same time. Don't!

Here is what Hilary also says: 'I think the big question for bohemians is using the alternative power they have in negotiations creatively – how do they put themselves in the other's shoes and work out how the other person values them – then use that power to up the power they have to get a good deal; it could be their uniqueness, their innovative approach. Too often, we assess what we think is our power and that undermines us in our own heads before we start. To get past this, we need to build trust and ask lots of questions to get understanding – as well as just negotiating the details.'

And here are his tips. They are almost Taoist in their approach. You must be like water in your negotiation: strong, but yielding; and somehow you must be completely unconcerned about the outcome. You must also be willing to be curious, creative and flexible. Hilary's approach, I think, is supremely bohemian.

1. **Don't ever negotiate with yourself.** I've watched teams sit in rooms and tell themselves they are too expensive and that the solution is to lower their price. This is nuts. Negotiate with what you observe and believe true when you are negotiating, not with what you convince yourself are your weak points. What *they* think of you matters, not what *you* think of you.

2. **Don't get too attached to a particular outcome.** If you are not prepared to walk away, you are powerless. Work out your options for walking away and develop them. It's a sure way of gaining power in the negotiation.

3. **Take your time.** If you are in a hurry to secure a deal and let others know it, you lose power. Ideally, you want them to be in a hurry and to need you.

4. **Put the relationship first.** Trust is the foundation for creative negotiation and being liked opens the door. The logic of your position is nothing like as important as whether you are trusted. Good relationships drive all the best deals.

5. **Do your planning, but be careful with your plans.** It's essential to work through what might happen, to have an outline strategy and prepare possible answers, but having a plan you expect to stick to makes you unresponsive when, ideally, you need to be curious and creative.

6. **Seek first to understand.** (And, as Stephen Covey, author of *The Seven Habits of Highly*

Effective People, says, then be understood.) You
know what you want, so why not listen and
understand what they want before you tell them
what it is? People need to be heard, and giving
this opportunity is an essential first step. You
don't have to agree with what the other party
says, but you can show them you understand
what they are saying.

7. **If the other party is still talking, they are still
negotiating.** The more talk, the more anger, the
more frustration, the more invested the other
party is. Watch their behaviour; don't just listen to
their words. The person to be fearful of is the one
who genuinely stops talking and leaves the room.

8. **Sugar the pill.** Saying to a child, 'What shall I
read you in bed?' is much more attractive than
'Time to go to bed.' What treat can you offer to
make your proposal more attractive?

9. **Give options.** As soon as you give the other
party options, they start evaluating which one is
best. It's a different focus, and it signals a
different, closing phase in negotiations.

10. **Signal that negotiations have come to an
end.** How does the other party know that you
have reached your breakpoint if you keep on
making offers? Make your final concessions
really small and then offer some alternative,
non-monetary, creative ones which, ideally, will
make the other party realize that the previous
offer was the best they are going to get.

11. **Fail sometimes.** Being right is a subjective judgement, and always having to be right kills creativity. In particular, if you are not losing some work – arguably, the figure is as high as a quarter of the amount of work you *are* getting – by being too expensive, your price is probably too low. If you are not prepared to take the risk of losing work, you are probably giving too much away.

Thank you, Hilary.

Now, we hear a lot today about teams: Team *Idler*; Team Nigella; Team Hodgkinson's Waste Solutions. It is easy to laugh at the word. But it says to me that there is a new way of creating a business, whereby the staff and the people you work with enjoy being a part of the process. But you must choose your team – and that could include your freelancers, suppliers, partners, investors, fellow directors, staff, managers – very carefully indeed, or disaster will ensue, as we discovered to our cost.

12. How to Choose Who You Work With

Of all the means to ensure happiness throughout the whole life, by far the most important is the acquisition of friends.
— Epicurus

As a creative entrepreneur, you will not be working alone. You will have collaborators, partners and, maybe, staff. All present their own challenges. In our case, with two directors and two staff, I often feel like I am trapped in a purgatorial collision between *This is Spinal Tap* and *Fawlty Towers*.

In the early days, our problem at the Idler Academy was that we did not know how to look after our staff properly, how to choose them in the first place, or how to get the best out of them. Employing people is tricky. You want to avoid being a bastardly boss, but the stress of starting up can be overwhelming, and you may take it out on your helpers. You begin to realize why there are thousands of books about management out there: it is a very difficult thing to do.

It's a bohemian issue. You want to be laid back and nice, but if you are too laid back then the people you work with will be laid back as well. They'll be late, they'll miss deadlines, they'll – in that lovely English phrase – 'take the piss'. So it would pay you to force yourself – perhaps against your better nature – to be very tough at the beginning.

The ideal that you are aiming for, as an amateur entrepreneur, is to surround yourself with professionals. Let them do the work while you think, go for walks, have meetings, make connections, raise money, give and hold talks, write books, make art, or whatever. This is simply good business practice, and I hear it again and again: get the professionals in. Or, as deceased publishing tycoon Felix Dennis put it, 'Find the talent. Hire the talent. Pay the talent.'

At the same time, you want to create a collaborative enterprise that is not based on competition and authority. A family, if you like. An organization with a small, central core which outsources much of its work to freelancers.

Now, the fundamental problem with having staff on the payroll, as opposed to employing freelancers, is that the interests of employer and employed are mis-aligned. The employee wants to put in the least amount of hours for the most amount of pay. And the employer wants to extract the maximum work from their staff for the smallest outlay. I'm not sure if the system works very well. It may be more honourable for both sides if we could all be freelancers instead. But that is not permitted: by law, if someone works for you in your shop or office, then they must be added to the payroll, and that means you have to give them five weeks' paid holiday a year, pay their taxes to the Inland Revenue direct, set up a payroll, and all sorts of other costly headaches. These problems tend not to occur when you use freelancers. Our relationships with our speakers and *Idler* contributors are easier to maintain. That's because they are our equals.

If you are thinking about employing staff, my advice would be to join the Federation of Small Businesses and read the legal documents relating to employment so that you understand what's involved.

The advice that follows about staff could apply to anyone with whom you are about to enter a working relationship: do your homework on them. Speak to other people who have worked with them. There are a lot of bullshitters out there who will be only too happy to take your money. And it's better, by the way, to employ staff who then become friends. When you employ friends as staff, it rarely ends well. As the wise Charles Handy said to me over lunch one day, 'When you go into business with a friend, you either lose the business or the friend.'

How We Did It All Wrong

Our first big problem was our name. The *Idler*. How can you tell your staff to work harder when you are telling the wider world to slack off? Our second mistake was to employ anyone who happened to be hanging around at the time and was fairly nice. You take them on without telephoning their references or even looking at a CV. Such people tend to be the unemployed children of your friends. Our third mistake was to assume that our staff would do exactly what we wanted them to without us having to tell them clearly exactly what that was. It is all too easy to reckon that, by some process of osmosis, they will do the job right. For example, I had my own particular way of setting out chairs for an event. I would ask someone else to do it, they would get it wrong, and then I'd move the chairs around in a badly disguised huff. What I should have done was to work out how I wanted the chairs to look, then created a system, and then told the staff member or volunteer how I wanted it done.

The management cliché here is 'They will do what you inspect, not what you expect.' So build in some sort of reporting system. Get them going on their KPIs. That's Key Performance Indicators, if you remember.

Another thing you will realize is that members of staff couldn't really give a toss about your business. They haven't borrowed fifty grand to get it going. They haven't put everything on the line. They can walk away if they feel like it. They will not understand how hard you are working in order to bring in the money that pays their wages. For five years, Victoria and I paid ourselves practically nothing from our business. We lived on royalties from my books, plus journalism, talks, Airbnb and government handouts. More than once I've had to dip into my personal overdraft to cover the monthly wage bill.

Bring these issues together and you have an unadulterated nightmare on your hands. I know, I've been there. Your staff think they're doing you a favour by turning up. You think you're doing them a favour by bunging them hundreds or thousands of pounds each month.

Our first staff member was a very intelligent and nice

person who was the unemployed son of a friend. We met a couple of times. Albert was public school and Oxbridge; very bright, very charming. Our plan was to make him number two to an experienced bookseller who had agreed to join our team. Unfortunately, the bookseller dropped out at the eleventh hour and we had to promote Albert to manager overnight. He did his best – in fact, he was invaluable and we had a lot of fun, but after a year or so he decided he'd had enough of us and moved to a remote Scottish island to devote his time to making electronic music and keeping hens. I wasn't too bothered that he was leaving because he'd caused me a lot of grief by being consistently late. I had sent him a text reading, 'The lateness must stop!' – not very *Idler*ish of me!

However, a short while after he left he sent me a long and abusive email about what a terrible boss I had been. I had micro-managed him, he said. He also complained about having to move furniture around and slagged us off to a mutual friend, which damaged our relationship with them.

There was I, wandering round in a state of pure self-deception, thinking that everybody loved me, whereas in fact they found me to be a total pain. It was David Brent again: trying to be a laid-back boss – and failing.

We then entered a second and much worse phase in our staffing story. Albert had brought along a few charming volunteers to help him at our evening events. When he left, we decided to employ some of them. They were nice people, clever; many of them had been to Marlborough and Bedales, top public schools. Tarquin, Damson and Fluffball, they were called.

'Why did you get sacked?' I asked one of our new help-ers, Tarquin, an out-of-work actor. He'd been working as a cleaner in a café nearby. 'Because I've got a personality, I suppose,' he replied.

Well, we would be much more enlightened than their previous employers, I thought, not thinking that there might in fact have been a reason why he had been sacked. Tarquin turned out to be a bit of a bad egg. In fact, I sacked him myself a few months later because he was out of control on drugs. He'd come and do a shift straight from a bender and would lose his temper with me.

Soon this little gang turned our beloved and costly busi-ness project into their own private playground. When you entered the shop, there would be an intimidating gaggle of big-headed Nancy Mitford wannabes lounging at the back of the shop, laughing. 'What is this – the junior common room?' asked one visitor, the head of a festivals chain. Cus-tomers began to complain. We started to notice that our wine stocks were diminishing with astonishing rapidity. One problem was that the Bedalians were completely unsuper-vised at weekends, because Victoria and I were two hundred miles away in our rented cottage in Devon. Gradually, it dawned on us that they were partying in the shop, smoking dope, taking ketamine and generally whooping it up.

They were fantastic company, and I liked them hugely as individuals. But they didn't have much of a work ethic. To take one example, they never cleaned the loo, though we would ask them to. They seemed to think that it was beneath them. 'Why am I cleaning the loo again?' I would ask myself. 'Isn't that what staff are for?'

To make matters worse, the girls were targeted by my divorced male friends and the shop became a sort of dating centre.

That second year, at least the first half of it, was the worst period in my life. Running a full-time bookshop, café and adult education centre – which doesn't at first sound like a stressful project; after all, I was hardly Philip Green – had put a massive strain on my relationship with Victoria, and it wasn't great for family life either. Had it all been a huge mistake? If it was, that was terrible, as we still had two years to go on the lease. I had a sort of mini-breakdown. I remember going for long walks on the Exmoor coast, sobbing as I went. What had happened to my old life as a full-time writer? Before we started our accursed shop, I used to get up each morning and go out on Exmoor thinking that I must be the luckiest man alive because I was earning a living doing something I loved. Now I woke up every morning full of self-pity, feeling like the most wretched soul that ever trod the earth.

My hands were far too full. I had ignored my own advice and overworked myself. At home, I was looking after three children on my own in our remote farmhouse while Victoria was in London. And I had no money. I was practically frozen with panic.

We somehow struggled on. Before he was sacked, Tarquin came to help us when we took out an area at festivals and was a complete pain in the arse, dancing on our café counter, falling asleep when he should have been working and generally repelling customers with his unwitty banter. I remember my friend Louis glancing over at our bookselling area one Sunday afternoon. Fluffball, barefoot, wearing a onesie, with stars on her cheeks and a whistle in her mouth, was standing on the counter, waving her arms in the air while Tarquin aimed pelvic thrusts in her direction.

Louis could hardly speak, so horror-struck was he: 'Your staff . . . your staff . . .' he said. It was like something out of *Heart of Darkness*.

When I told my mother that our shop had been turned into Party Central, she said, helpfully, 'When the cat's away . . .'

Things Improve – but not before the Police Get Involved

Luckily, we found Julian Mash, a bookshop manager of many years' standing, and he joined us as manager. This time, I did follow up references, study his CV and interview him – employment basics which we'd neglected to follow with our previous lot.

Well, Julian cleared out the charming-but-useless mob. Almost overnight, they stopped hanging around the shop. We moved on to a new phase – but not before one major crisis.

I had banned Tarquin from the shop. We suspected him of drinking our wine and stealing books, and he'd certainly behaved like a complete idiot. And I didn't want him leading Damson astray. She was sweet, but easily influenced.

When Julian started, we forked out £500 on a nice laptop for him. He came in one Tuesday morning and said that he couldn't find it – which was odd, because we'd hidden it carefully in the basement. I called Damson and asked if she'd seen it anywhere. She said she hadn't.

My son Arthur, then aged eleven, tracked the computer using 'find my iphone'. We located it to a college campus just outside London. I told Damson this, but she didn't react. Then Victoria remembered that Tarquin had told her over the summer that he was off to this particular college to study acting. We'd nailed him.

I think Damson probably tipped him off, because when we contacted him he told us that he no longer had the computer. He admitted having stolen it and, in an astonishing email, claimed that he had taken it by mistake. 'When I unpacked at college, I saw I had two laptops, and I thought: Oh, what good karma.' We said that we'd forgive him if he gave us the money for the computer, but he refused. We reported him to the police, who went to see him but took no action. They wrote to us to say that Tarquin had 'thrown the computer in the river, where it now remains'. It seems that you can steal up to £500 worth of stuff and get off scot-free.

Damson was in our bad books for having colluded in Tarquin's theft. She'd let Tarquin into the shop, knowing he was banned. So she left, too. Julian had saved us and became our staff manager as well as our shop manager. The difference is, perhaps, that we were paying him a proper wage, whereas the young people were on barely above minimum wage. You get what you pay for, I suppose.

In the end, although Tarquin was clearly a wrong 'un, the rest of them were perfectly nice kids but we had no idea how to train them or make them work well for us. I think now that this was all partly due to a lack of confidence on our part: we were so pleased and grateful that anyone would want to help us that we failed to follow the basic rules. Like many bohemians, I assumed that the rules didn't apply to me. That I would be able to manage staff just by being nice. All our mistakes and a lot of pain could have been very easily avoided, and I could have saved myself a year of hell, if we'd just followed some very simple business employment procedures.

Again, it may feel unnatural and awkward to the freedom-loving bohemian to follow the dictates of management gurus. But doing things the proper way could save you a lot of headaches. Once you have learned the conventional route, then you can start to improvise. But not before.

The Proper Way

We invited James Reed, the chairman of reed.co.uk, to give a talk to our business-course group. His advice sounds simple, but is not easy to carry out. It is: 'Find the right people. Let them get on with it.'

I have heard versions of this piece of wisdom again and again, and it is completely true. My life became manageable once we followed it. The absolute ideal is not to have to manage, motivate and assess your staff, because they do it themselves, leaving you free to concentrate on strategy. As one of Charles Handy's friends said to him, 'If you get the right people to start with, and they know what to do, then they get on with it themselves.' I have a liking for a management book called *Do Nothing*, whose author argues that entrepreneurs should be continually aiming towards a state of doing nothing. That would be the sign that they have created the ultimate team and system.

That is clearly the key to everything. That is the way of the idle manager. Another book of business advice advises, 'Get the right people in the right seats.' If you manage to do that, then idleness will follow. And, once you have found the right people, look after them. John Brown adds, 'Hold annual appraisals with staff. Tell them what is going well and what is not, and ask them to do the same to you.'

Charlie Gladstone has 120 members of staff. 'It's quite a lot, but they are all fantastic and I know and like them all. I think that the secret here is to like people and to employ managers who like people, too. If you meet your staff with genuine interest and affection, they will respond accordingly. It seems that the key things are to remain constant, professional and caring. Praise is oxygen, but people also need to understand clearly when they have not come up to scratch. And it's important to set high standards and live up to them yourself.'

Get things wrong, and you could be piling up a lot of grief for yourself. Here are a few basic rules to follow:

1. Check references by phone

However wonderful your prospective staff member appears to be in interview, and however perfectly suited to your job, you must always phone their references. A former boss will tell the truth. Ask about their time-keeping and their honesty.

Ask whether they can take orders. One of the worst things about our year with our young employees was that they were incapable of doing, or too big-headed to do, what they were told. It's an age thing: I remember being exactly the same when I was their age. Big-headed but without any ability. And, of course, neither did I have any idea how to tell them to do stuff. I found it embarrassing.

You should do a bit of background work on potential partners, collaborators and consultants as well. Can you phone up someone else who has worked with this person? That way, you'll discover any issues pretty quickly.

2. Teach them

In an ideal world, you will hire people who are better at what you want them to do than you are. But you will also have to teach them what it is specifically that you want them to do and how you want them to do it: you need to take some time out for staff training. Our example was mail order. I just let our staff get on with it in their own way, without bothering to teach them how to do it properly, or even how to create a good mail-order system. You may laugh, but mail order is a real art, and more difficult than it looks. After Tarquin left, we started to receive complaints that customers had not received what they had ordered. I've had this countless times: staff leave and, lacking any sense of responsibility, they just stuff a load of orders in a drawer and forget about them. So if you do end up with well-meaning but clueless young volunteers, as we often did, do not be fooled into thinking that they know what they are doing, however breezily and confidently they act in front of you. Monitor them closely.

Create a system, or be enslaved by another man's! Even with Julian, I had to spend a couple of days working out a decent mail-order system, which I then wrote down in steps, printed out and put in a folder. Once I'd put in that two days, though, he and the other staff got on with it fine. It's important to write your systems down clearly, because you never know who may be working in the shop. You might be ill, your most experienced staff member may be ill, and so it is no good if one person knows where everything is but has made no note of it.

The more of your processes and systems you have written down, the better it is. This actually adds value to your company. It means that anyone can come in and do the job. We now use Google Docs non-stop to detail information and processes.

3. Do not use free job sites

We once used an absolutely terrible mainstream job-hunting site which I cannot name here. We advertised for a bookshop assistant and we had one stipulation: they should have experience of working in a bookshop. Of the two hundred or so applications we received, not a single one had been sent by someone who had worked in a bookshop. Ninety per cent of the applications were illiterate and most of the applicants had clearly cut and pasted their CV together from examples on the Internet. Some had not even read over their CV: many had repeated vast blocks of text. Extraordinary: you wonder what on earth schools are doing. One last point is that, according to their own CVs, these kids were all going to be the next Steve Jobs: they were great leaders but also fantastic at working in a team. They were self-confident, motivated, customer-facing, innovative, hard-working, punctual . . . and streams of other hyperbolically laudatory epithets. When you looked at their work experience, though, they'd generally done two weeks in an Oxfam shop. The whole exercise was a complete and utter waste of time.

Our good staff have come via word of mouth, or have contacted us out of the blue. Recently, we did a project with a marketing person. I called both her referees and had a nice chat with them. They were hugely enthusiastic about her, so we could carry on with total confidence.

You should advertise on your website and tell newsletter subscribers that you are looking for people. Or use a decent recruitment consultant like Reed. That would be the way to find the professionals.

4. Accept that you are the boss

It has taken me a while to accept that I am the leader of this organization which I have created – in other words, that I must take responsibility for everything that goes wrong and give credit to other people for everything that goes right. I think I keep hoping that a new partner or staff member will sort out my problems, but they never do.

This is an important realization. It means you have to grow up. You are not everyone's pal. You are their employer.

In *Mutiny on the Bounty*, the tyrannical Captain Bligh is asked by an officer whether he is going to go and join the party on Tahiti. He says that he isn't: 'You can hardly expect obedience from last night's partner in debauch.'

The whole point of Bligh is that he is a terrible leader – his crew mutiny, choosing permanent exile from England over submission to his might. But still . . . a little bit of distance between owner and staff might be a good thing. James Reed says that leadership is lonely.

And how to lead? Well, as you know, there are reams of books on this subject, and people go off on three-year courses to study how to lead. So, here, I'll just offer a few thoughts.

1. Create a common goal

The most important thing, I think, is to communicate a shared purpose and make everyone feel that they are doing something worthwhile. You have to keep repeating this 'mission statement', whether in conversation, or by writing it on the wall in huge letters, or appending it to your emails. That makes it fun. In our case, it's a simple matter of improving people's lives with fun teaching.

Another piece of good leadership advice is to see only

the good in people. You should relentlessly focus on what they are good at, ignore the bad and not try to control them or force them in the wrong direction. Clearly, there are going to be rows and, clearly, you will occasionally get a real wrong 'un, like Tarquin, who must simply be removed from your life, business and indeed world completely.

But the most fruitful way to lead people is to bring out the best in them and, as far as possible, get them doing what they naturally enjoy and are good at. Of course, the dirty work also has to be done. Someone is going to have to clean the loo and wash the dishes. So you need a system to deal with that. Maybe you can sort out a rota. The leader should lend a hand and be ready to take orders from the manager he has appointed. I am quite happy to take orders from Bobbie at an event: after all, I have asked her to organize it, so it is now up to her to manage it.

The principle is this: with both your staff and business partners, you should either sack them or love them. There should be no halfway house. That is not a particularly easy thing to achieve, because we are all addicted to moaning. 'It's more fun to say bad stuff about someone than good stuff,' said my son, Henry, who is ten, the other day. 'That's not good, though, Henry, is it?' I said. To which he replied: 'It's a fact.'

When it comes to leadership, Charles Handy says that, in his view, it boils down to the following mantra: 'Know yourself, know where you want to go, know your people, be humble and listen.'

Avoid gossip. And I say that as one of the worst

offenders. My big, non-stop, chatterbox mouth has got me into trouble many times, and I am trying to learn to keep it shut. When your staff complain about each other, try not to get drawn in. Rise above it. Do not listen to the whingeing. Point out the good aspects of the person they are complaining about. They will follow your lead.

2. Obey the conventions

I read a very useful business book which recommended drawing a diagram of your management structure. Give each person a box, a title and a list of their areas of responsibility. For example:

1. Tom: vision; money-raising; editing magazine; PR; sleeping
2. Victoria: implementation; developing new business relationships; going to cocktail parties; marketing
3. Julian: sales; ad sales; managing the magazine; website sales
4. Bobbie: events; customer management; fielding customer complaints

The point is that the system you need is similar for all businesses, no matter what they are selling. Work out what each person is supposed to do, and don't blur the lines. Delegate. Charles Handy points out that delegation is not the same as giving orders. Delegation means handing the responsibility for a whole chunk of the work to someone else and letting them get on with it.

3. Laugh

When it comes to the people you work with, laugh at them, laugh with them and let them laugh at you. Above all, you need to keep thinking that 'nothing really matters'. Doubtless, the precursor to my own mini-breakdown was an escalating sense of my own importance on this planet. Probably the best management or business-advice book you could read would be *The Wisdom of Insecurity* by the fifties 'spiritual entertainer' and promoter of Eastern philosophy in the west Alan Watts. For anyone aspiring to become a Zen entrepreneur, that is a good one to keep by your bedside.

A Note on Meetings

It's fashionable to criticize meetings and see them as being a waste of time. I don't agree with that. I think they are essential. I love chatting to people. And without regular meetings, you can lose track of what is going on in your business.

We have a weekly team meeting at the same time, on the same day, every week. There is no excuse not to turn up. We try to keep it down to forty-five minutes and divide it into three sections. The first is to talk about the figures from the previous week and the previous month. Compare them with the previous year's equivalent. Other figures could include KPIs, for example, newsletter sign-ups, Twitter followers, new products, PR mentions. The second is to make plans for the forthcoming week and weeks, to apportion tasks and report back on tasks undertaken in previous weeks. The third section is to address any issues or problems. This is the time to bring up anything that went wrong. Force everyone to come up with at least two problems. The one thing you don't want to hear is that everything is going fine.

You should welcome issues and problems as a chance to make improvements. The successful entrepreneur must not get stressed out when things go wrong. You must actively enjoy disaster.

Even your enemies can be friends in disguise, as we will now find out . . .

13. How to Deal with Enemies

'Tis the first art of kings, the power to suffer hate.
— Seneca the Younger

To you, your business, project or scheme is completely harmless. After all, what's wrong with selling organic pork pies, luxury marshmallows, ideas for idling, grammar lessons, vintage clothing or selling American cereals in East London? Everyone will like you and praise you for what you are doing, surely? How could you possibly arouse envy, resentment, hatred or trolling on Twitter? It's not like you're displacing indigenous communities and drilling for oil in your relentless quest for riches, or encouraging poor people to go into debt by lending them money at vast interest rates so you can dig a basement in your Notting Hill mansion.

But whatever you do, however apparently innocuous, someone out there will enjoy hating you. And you have to let them have their fun.

Some of my haters appeared on Amazon, writing reviews of my books. 'This book,' observes one 'Amy Kitten' of my second book, *How to be Free*, 'is poorly written playground psychology. It is just a vast array of self-indulgent fluff ... Drab, shallow and hideously dull . . . nothing can mask the desperate plea for acceptance in his work.' Ooh, Miss Kitten!

Many readers and other amateur critics will accuse you of the cardinal sin of trying to make money, as does 'MacUser', when commenting on my book *How to be Idle*: 'Why, after all, must we be taught to be idle? Surely real idleness would have been not to write the book at all, but that would have spoilt a nice little earner.' Ha! Got me there. Clever.

'I wish I had the author's gift for words to describe how terrible this book is,' adds 'Johann28'. 'He's basically one of those people who's made an awful load of money and now feels he has the right to preach to us about simplifying our lives.' I'm not quite sure where Johann28 has got his information about my balance sheet from, but he's wrong there, I'd say.

Sometimes, though, you have to concede that Amazon reviewers have a point: 'I was hoping for an uplifting book about how to feel free and live a life of value,' said 'Janeonthemoon'. 'It turned out to be a very depressing book by a man making excuses for his disorganized lifestyle.'

Wow – how did she know that about me?

Whatever you do, you will attract enemies. And they won't hold back. Thanks to the Internet, they can send their comments, which perhaps should have stayed in the safety of the pub, out into the public realm. They can get drunk at home and then send their biting aperçus out into the social-media sphere. When we decided to open the

Idler Academy, one of my enemies went on to a forum to complain about our project. 'Have you seen that Hodge is opening a horribly twee little cake shop in Notting Hill?' trumpeted the anonymous troll. (My enemies on this site liked to call me Hodge, which, by the by, was eighteenth-century slang for a poor farmer.) 'Let's throw Molotov cocktails through the window on their opening night,' the troll went on to propose. Luckily, he did not appear to have much success in drumming up an anti-*Idler* army and our opening night went by without incident.

Just today, after sending out an email complaining about the huge number of £100,000 Range Rovers in west London, I received this from someone calling themselves Henry Porter (not, one assumes from the faulty grammar, the distinguished journalist):

> range rovers – notting hill what do you do with your money . . . escape the city and go to your farm . . . ? your just another carpet bagger . . . family wealth or did you 'idle' as a stockbroker and help those rovers accumulate more of london's wealth . . . how does anybody 'idle' when the lot of us beggars are getting corn-holed every minute . . .
>
> the city of london and the bankers who own it are destroying the planet, along with bend-it pass go and go straight to hell along with the rest of your piss ant [sic] rich idlers . . .

I suppose I only have myself to blame, though, for some of this hostility. First, if you question consumerism in your work, then some wag will always delight in saying, 'But I saw you coming out of Tesco!' It goes with the territory. Crass, who inspired a generation to take responsibility for their own lives, once turned up to play a gig (for which they charged an entrance fee of something like £1 waged, 50 pence unwaged) and found that someone had written, 'CRASS – CAPITALIST WANKERS' on the dressing-room wall.

The other point to make is that you should, as Rudyard Kipling so wisely advised, treat those two impostors, triumph and disaster, just the same. Enemies can help you to make improvements, as long as you can sort out the time-wasters and cranks from those with a genuine criticism.

When Customers Turn

So you try to get sensible about money so that your children can have shoes. But then you start being attacked for being a breadhead. Because you have espoused bohemian principles like not being interested in money, rejecting consumerism and lying in bed at strange times, your fans get cross.

'Dear Mr Hodgkinson,' ran an email I received recently from a German *Idler* reader. 'You have turned into a busy little capitalist shopkeeper. It's all sell, sell, sell. Please unsubscribe me from your newsletter.'

Er . . . yeah? How do you think I am supposed to live? Even the most hardcore lefty has to sell stuff. I feel like saying to these people, Great: send me some money and I'll stop selling. Believe me, I'd be very happy sitting in a Devon farmhouse writing and reading and letting other people do the selling, if I could afford to do that.

Other readers have written to us to say, 'Stay small, how we like you' or 'I can't believe you have moved to London.' So they were happy when we were living on nothing and working fourteen hours a day, but if we ever made a profit, they would consider that to be a sell-out. We are trying to make a living doing what we do. Boff Whalley of anarcho-popsters Chumbawumba, who were accused of selling out by their fans, remembers that it was common for anarchists to run a small record company that deliberately avoided making a profit – while keeping a job working for Barclays. Absurd.

Having said all that, I am aware of some of the contradictions. My books counsel independence from big business. I had written long articles attacking moneylenders – now called bankers – for charging high rates of interest on loans, a process that used to be condemned by all right-thinking people as usury before around 1500. I even lectured on the subject on the steps of St Paul's at the invitation of the Occupy protesters. And now I was borrowing money from a bank – or trying to. One week in my newspaper column I attempted a gag on this issue: I rejected usury, I quipped, and now usury has rejected me.

I had urged my readers to smash the system but was now finding that I was entering the system. The problem is, if you want a retail outlet or a venue, you are forced to play by the rules. Yes, you could squat, but what has happened to all the noble 'free school' ideas that came out of Occupy? Precisely nothing. They take over a building, put on some terrible lectures about the male gaze, get chucked out, write a manifesto, then go and get a job at some horrific middle-class rentier system masquerading as a charity. Whereas if you pay a landlord, pay staff and sell stuff, you have more freedom.

Many readers attacked us for high ticket prices. Unless you have a business selling beer, which even the unwaged will happily spend a fortune on, then some wit somewhere will always accuse you of profiteering. I am always amazed how people will complain about paying to see one of our events and then blow fifty quid in the pub without thinking about it.

A tip here is to offer concessions to the unwaged, and to students and pensioners. Surprisingly few people take up the concession price, and the knockers are unable to knock you.

In addition to committing the crime of writing books about idleness and freedom, I made things worse by actively upsetting my core fan base. Some years ago, I set up a forum on the *Idler*'s website. It was a free area (free to its visitors – I had to pay to have it set up and maintained). *Idler* readers came on to it and discussed relevant issues. For a while I found it to be a pleasant distraction. I enjoyed contributing to the debates on the best way to grow tomatoes, and meeting readers online.

One morning, sitting in my study in Devon, I opened our forum and found the following comment from an anonymous poster: 'I've said it before, and I'll say it again.

Hodgkinson is full of shit.' Others said things like, 'It's all right for him, with his Cambridge education' or 'It's all right for him, with all his money.'

Hmm. That's not very nice. I thought this was supposed to be a fan site. I tried to ignore it, but in the end I found I was not thick-skinned enough to take the continuing abuse. I got fed up with it and decided to close the site down.

Then I made a mistake which I regret to this day. I told the forum people to 'spew their *bon mots* elsewhere'. It was a phrase that author Douglas Coupland had used in 1993 when I interviewed him for the *Idler*. The people who had posted on the forum, having dished out the abuse themselves, did not much like being on the receiving end and stormed off in a huff.

One of them moved the whole thing over to a new website, which they called the Idle Foundation, like the 'real IRA', and that was in fact a good solution. A few used it to abuse me, but then other members would defend me. Again, a stoic attitude was required. I had to remind myself of the old adage 'When you stick your head above the parapet, people are likely to take pot shots at you.' If you throw provocative ideas out into the world, then you can't expect everyone to agree with you.

Others get worse abuse than I do. My friend the conductor Charles Hazlewood, who tirelessly communicates the joys of classical music on TV and radio, runs orchestras in South African townships and put together the Paraorchestra for the Olympics, for practically no money, has to cope with the fact that some numbskull with too much time on his hands started a forum thread called 'Charles Hazlewood is a cunt'. Here is a sample quote from that same critical discussion: 'He's a cock who thinks serious music can be "popularised" by saying things such as "Purcell sounds like Dizzee Rascal" and "The Prodigy sound like Mahler."'

The thing about abuse like this is that, rightly considered, it is actually flattering. It means that people are talking about you. So just keep going. The more events you organize, the more articles you post on your website, the lower down the page the online abuse will sink. And although it's tempting when assaulted with witless fury to pen a clever quip in response, in general, the knockers, or 'haters', are best ignored.

Having said that, I will admit that, sometimes, I break this rule and I write back. And, occasionally, I have found that if I engage with these attacks, the attacker appreciates the attention and accepts your response. So you can turn an attacker into a fan. We recently received an email from a woman, a fan of my books, who had been inspired by them to move out of the city and was living on a farm with little money and her young family. She was dismayed that I had now moved back to London and was trying to sell books and courses through our Academy project. She also objected to the fact that we now had a former hedge-fund manager advising us. Victoria and I wrote a long letter to her explaining how all this had happened – no book deals; children growing up; Christian the hedgie had grown so bored and stressed by his job that he had decided to quit to help small businesses like us. And she wrote a lovely letter back.

The Basil Fawlty Syndrome

Becoming a shopkeeper was not easy. I thought that making and serving coffees would be fun, but it wasn't. I had gone from being a self-indulgent writer to being an outward-facing customer-services representative. I tried to be as cheerful as possible while making hot drinks for snooty customers. But I felt my aggrieved ego swelling up. 'Don't you know who I am?' I wanted to say, when they complained that the coffee was cold. 'I am a published author! My books are available in twenty countries. I am huge in the Czech Republic!' I soon turned into Basil Fawlty, trying to be a good host but somehow feeling it was all beneath me.

On one occasion, we'd had an unusually busy Sunday because we'd had a great bit of press. A couple with a child came in, sat down and ordered a coffee. We made the mother one using our pour-over, slow-filter method. On leaving and paying, she said, 'The coffee was cold.' I explained that the coffee was not supposed to be very hot; it was the new trend in coffee culture: drip coffee. In fact, there had been a big piece about it in the paper. That will be five pounds please, madam. And here are a couple of *Idler* badges for you, by way of an apology.

The next day I was horrified to read the following review on a popular website: 'A terrible place. Uncomfy chairs and cold coffee. When I complained, the pretentious manager gave me a lecture about an article in the *Evening Standard* and how cold coffee was trendy. He charged us full price for the coffees then gave me a badge with a snail on it. What a lunatic.'

Sometimes, You Should Listen

My first reaction on getting abuse and complaints is generally what I feel is righteous and defensive fury. But after a while Victoria and I realized that we ought to listen to the complaints. In complaining, your customers may well be giving you ideas for improving things. Maybe they've got a point. And for every one who voices a complaint, there are probably one hundred who are thinking it. The complaint above led us to change our coffee-making methods so that the punters got hot coffee.

So if you get a bad review, don't worry about it. Just think: this has been sent here by God to help me improve things. And the *Idler* readers who complain about the way I appear to have abandoned my principles: well, maybe they can help me to evolve my philosophy, as well.

So unless the whingers are clearly lunatics and simply nasty – in which case they should be cut out of your life – then listen to their complaints. They have been sent there by fate to help you tackle a certain problem. And write back to them with as much courtesy as you can muster. And if you do make the mistake of working on the shop floor in retail, then the solution is to put on a performance. To act. Whatever you do, don't take it personally.

Former Staff

You might also find that former staff will slag you off. We have a few disgruntled ex-staff members who were disappointed by the fact that a job at the Idler Academy is hard work and involves, well, working. So, out there somewhere, I am fairly certain that there is a group of charming, clever, young Sebastian Flytes saying things like: 'What nonsense that whole *Idler* thing is. I worked there and I had to move furniture around and clean the floor while the owners sipped claret in the garden with their smart friends!' or 'Yes, Oscar. Anarchists? Paf! They are merely capitalist mill-owners in hippy garb. And the idea that they support young writers? Tom never took the slightest interest in my blog.'

I have even speculated on the existence of a support group of former Academy workers who have been in some way traumatized by their experience. I believe that such organizations exist for Starbucks. Julian, our manager, regularly threatens that he is going to start a union for the Idle Workers of the World (IWOW), and demand higher wages.

Generally, when people attack you, it is down to resentment. They wish that they'd had the courage to do what you are doing. The next best thing is to run you down. So ignore the haters. Move on. Keep working.

Enemies among Your Nearest and Dearest

You always hurt the one you love, says the song, and if you go into business with your partner, spouse, boyfriend, girlfriend, friend, whatever, your relationship is going to be sorely tested. My business partner is my wife, Victoria.

This is not easy. On the plus side, you are never bored. It is in fact great to have a joint project with your partner. We chatter away about everything and we can share the pains and joys of the process.

On the downside, you're introducing a huge amount of new potential argument material into your life. You can now argue about money, staff, stock, marketing, who does what and so on.

I have been asked many times what it's like working with Victoria. The answer is that it is a complete nightmare. Because she is always right. My friend Matthew calls his wife 'the truth', and that is what it feels like with Victoria. We will disagree about something violently at the time. Later, while lying in bed, I will think about it and realize – Oh, she's right. Dammit.

She gleefully points out my faults – that's another irritating habit. I talk too much in meetings; I ramble; I don't listen to people. Also, I am deaf, insensitive, lazy, don't earn enough money and don't play football with my children. 'I've just realized,' she said to me one day recently in a tone of triumph: 'You're an idiot!'

Why can't she just tell me how wonderful I am all day long? And praise everything I do?

There is a very human temptation to blame the other person when things go wrong. For example, when our staff complained about me, Victoria didn't exactly leap to my defence. She was just glad that someone else had seen the reality of how awful I was, and she was no longer on her own in this. 'You see? You really are an idiot and a tosser – it's not just me.'

And when things go wrong, I try to blame Victoria, naturally. I remember screaming at her down the phone at certain points during the first couple of years we were in business. 'Why does everyone ask me to do everything?' I would holler. Another thing that annoys me: Victoria seems to think that I am a 24/7 walking tech-consultant centre who has memorized every single one of her passwords.

When we're putting on an event and the projector doesn't work, who is the tech guy?

Yes. Me.

So you can see why I find working with her so difficult. I consulted Charles Handy and his wife, Elizabeth, on this issue. The couple have worked together for forty years: he writes the books and she does the business – what she calls the 'back office'. I told her that Victoria had been complaining that I didn't give her enough credit for what she did. 'Charles doesn't give me enough credit!' she said. 'You must. You must thank her often in private and you must thank her in public as well.' The Handys reckoned that working couples should sit down, perhaps with a mediator, and create a workable system in order to avoid arguments. The key thing, they reckoned, was to make sure that each party knows what they are supposed to be doing. Keep the roles separate. Write out your job description. And rather than wait for a crisis to blow up, it is much better simply to schedule regular meetings, with a time limit, an agenda and minutes – yes, even with your husband, or wife, or partner. This may feel unnatural at first, but it's essential.

Something else to bear in mind if you are working with your other half is that you run the risk of your home becoming a second office, and all your children hear you talk about is business. I met the husband-and-wife team behind one of Britain's best bookshops, Jaffé and Neale. When I mentioned this issue, they said they knew exactly what I was talking about. They said that they invent strict rules to avoid excessive business chat in front of their kids.

I try not to worry too much about this and hope that the entrepreneurial spirit may rub off on the children. However, it's something I have discussed with Victoria, and both of us steer clear of the subject at the dinner table. One thing I do regret is moaning about being poor in front of the children, as both of us did non-stop during the first two or three years, while we were still living in Devon. Our children, rightly, were probably a little mystified as to why we would want to spend so much time and energy worrying about something that did not seem to earn any money.

Having said all this, partners are great sounding boards. They stop you from doing stupid things. They put a brake on your crazy ideas. As Bill Drummond said, 'It's a little known fact that your best mate is a genius.'

Due to Victoria's constant questioning, dialogue and complaint, we approach the truth and slowly approach wisdom – or at least manage to make some sort of decision. My behaviour slowly improves. And so does the business. Without her, there would always lurk the danger of me turning into some sort of horrific, egotistical dictator.

Your Friends are Not Your Customers

This brings me on to my final point. Friends, you may find, are not always good for business. Certainly, you should never rely on them. And never expect them to be good customers.

We assumed that all our friends would flock to our coffee shop, buy books, hang out there and generally thank us for providing a sophisticated cultural hub. But no: their view was that they didn't want to give us any of their money. Once, when I sent a mail-out advertising some evening talks which I was hosting, one friend wrote back, 'Thank you for the spam. I don't see you enough, anyway, and now you are asking me to pay for the privilege.' On inspecting our list of 'unsubscribes' to this same mailing list, we would often find the names of our closest friends. That hurt.

Some friends did come to our events but would not pay. They considered that getting in for free and drinking all our booze was a supportive act. (If any of our friends are reading this, I am not talking about you. I am talking about different friends.)

Victoria and I soon realized that there is a lesson to be learned here, so we created our own adage: 'Friends are not your market.' Don't expect anything of your friends: your market is real people who you don't already know. In any case, you don't really want their orders. They're not real. Johnny Boden of the eponymous children's clothing brand said in an interview that in his first year of trading he got a few of what he called 'sympathy orders' from friends but in the second year all those orders vanished, leaving him without a business. So there is a risk that orders from friends will be seen as evidence of a wider demand. When it isn't.

Friends and relatives will also spew forth torrents of clueless advice: 'You really should sell more children's books'; 'You really should get a coffee machine'; 'You really should do more marketing'; 'You're too expensive.' Unless your advisors actually have experience in running a burger stand, or coffee shop, or event venue, or PR company, or whatever it is that you are doing, then their advice can be safely discounted.

So my advice is to keep your friends as friends. Do not try to make them into customers. For one thing, they might resent it, and for another, their custom is unlikely to be sustainable. And then you will worry: do they really like what you are doing or are they just trying to be nice? Instead, find real customers: the people who love what you do.

Being an independent operator in the digital age can be

exhausting and dispiriting because there always seems so much to do. The Internet is a hungry beast and devours your content. There is always an improvement to be made. So the bohemian can very easily make the cardinal error of turning into a workaholic, which was not the point at all. Now let us look at how to avoid that trap.

14. Never, Ever Overwork

Without a considerable amount of leisure man is cut off from many of the best things.
— Bertrand Russell

It seems that virtually every business book I read tells me not to overwork. In the early days of the Idler Academy, though, it seemed impossible to avoid doing fourteen- or even sixteen-hour days. There was an avalanche of stuff to do. And things went wrong constantly. They call it firefighting. As things went on, we found more suitable staff and we got better at managing, too. We improved our systems.

As I keep saying in this book, being chaotic is not charming and it is not bohemian. It will just waste you a lot of time. Instead, what you should do is sit down and work out a system which will help you to enjoy what you are doing and which gives you plenty of freedom for long walks. In other words, you will be able to be idle – which is good, because idleness is creatively fertile and also good for your health – if you are efficient.

When we improved our efficiency by writing down our systems, developing our own 'way', this gave us more time for reflection out of the office and for meetings, reading and going out to events and dos. Everything that your senses take in goes into the compost bin of your mind and is turned over and transformed at some point into some useful idea or insight. So you must keep wandering around the city and the countryside. You must keep reading and listening to music. You must make time for doing nothing.

Doing nothing, apart from being justified in a business sense, is also good for your body and your soul. If you manage to get enough sleep, enough exercise and enough time just staring out of the window, then your health will remain strong.

If you kill yourself with worry and overwork, you will become unhealthy, unhappy and a pain in the arse to the people you live with and the people you work with. 'Govern a great nation as you would cook a small fish,' says Lao Tzu. 'Do not overdo it.' Overwork is for stupid people and slaves. We businesslike bohemians and bohemian businesspeople are efficient.

Take Time with Your Correspondence

One obvious example of taking it slowly is that you should be very careful not to be in too much of a hurry with your emails and indeed with Twitter. Do not, in general, send emails after seven in the evening, when you may have had a drink. Do not reply to difficult or aggressive emails before consulting your wise counsellors. Wait a few hours. I think it's a good idea to send some sort of reply as quickly as you can, something like 'Noted with thanks and I'll get back to you asap'; that's just good manners. When you leave an email unanswered, you sow the seed of worry in the other person's mind. But you may need time to ponder if the email requires it.

Should we slow down when writing emails? I used to try to add a few mannerly embellishments to mine, like 'Yours faithfully' and 'I remain, sir, your humble servant' and 'My dearest and sincerest wish is that this email finds you in rude health and good spirits.' Which is fun. But email is by nature a brusque medium, probably better suited to writing short notes. The medium is the message, and the email medium says: 'Busy busy busy!' I know that some business types are so scatty they will simply not read a long email. They would perhaps rather have a face-to-face meeting, Skype or make a telephone call.

I have found lately that my attempts at old-world for-mality when composing emails have failed completely and my emails have degenerated into breathless, typo-strewn streams of verbiage sans capital letters, sans punctuation, sans anything much of the old world. This is a bit sad; but then, I could always write a good old-fashioned letter instead. And on the rare occasions when I do sit down to write a letter, I really delight in the process; the ink, the paper, and so on. But it does seem like a bit of an effort. 'Letters, no way,' says my friend Gav. 'You've got to find paper, pen, an envelope, look up the address, find a stamp, go to a postbox. Just so much hassle.' But so nice to receive. I guess the only letters that are written these days are thank-you letters from children to their grand-parents. (And they do like receiving them so I think it is worth forcing children to do it.)

More Sleep Required

'Sleep on it' really is good advice. You should never make big decisions when you are tired. When Victoria suddenly raises some thorny business issue at ten o'clock at night, I risk her fury and try to postpone dealing with it until the following morning, when my brain will actually be awake and I can see clearly. Evenings are good for reading, chatting, dreaming, drinking, nodding off and talking rubbish. They are not good for business.

The Importance of Routine

My friend Alan once said to me about my book-writing routine, 'I suppose you write when the inspiration takes you.' And his wife sagely corrected him: 'Inspiration would take Tom down the pub.'

I find that, as a self-employed person, I need to impose some sort of routine on myself. Without the bells of matins to summon you to your prayers or labours, you need to be the boss of yourself. Personally, I need about four hours to work on my own each day. I tried to work every morning at home but found there were too many distractions. I don't have a study with a door I can shut. My desk is in the TV room, where the children play. Victoria wanders in and asks me for a password. Sick children watch Japanese animations on the telly.

Being naturally lazy and easily distracted, I have to be

very disciplined. My aim is to create a monk-like routine. So I decided to spend every morning from nine till one on my own with the laptop in a café. Luckily, there is a great café attached to our local theatre, the Bush, which is a mere five-minute walk from my front door. Since finding the Bush Theatre, a former library, I have been way more productive and way happier.

One difficulty is that the laptop itself throws up a myriad of distractions. Right now, I can count ten, most of which can be excused as work-related: Facebook, *Idler* orders, LinkedIn, the *Guardian* website, Google Analytics, YouTube ukulele tutorial for 'Here Comes the Sun', email, the position of my books on Amazon . . . So, during my four-hour stint, I will quit my mail program for an hour or two at a time and also quit my web browser. That way I can actually get some writing and thinking done.

It must have been easy for the Edwardian gentleman to work. You opened your post over breakfast and read *The Times*. Then you retired to your study to read, write letters and think, and emerged at one o'clock. No telephone. Cook will have prepared your meal. No washing-up. Then out for a stroll with the dog before returning to your study and dropping off in front of the fire that someone else has laid and a whisky handed to you by the maid.

However, it seems that no less a poet than T. S. Eliot forced a routine on himself, though he managed only three hours a day of actual writing and worked not from a café but from an office at Faber and Faber, where he was a director. He said: '[C]omposition of any length . . . means for me regular hours, say ten to one. I found that three hours a day is about all I can do of actual composing. I could do the polish perhaps later.' And it was the same for Graham Greene. He would work from eight till eleven every day, and then would drink his first cocktail. No more work. Sounds ideal.

Café as Friend to the Creative Entrepreneur

Just to make a quick detour from our central subject here: it occurs to me that it is easier than ever today to be a bohemian in business because you can work from cafés, thanks to Broadband and handy plugs. This means that you can stay in the hubbub of life while working, exactly like those trend-setting, chain-smoking bohemians Jean-Paul Sartre and Simone de Beauvoir, who, as I hardly need remind you, worked in artistic hangout Les Deux Magots on St-Germain-des-Prés, as had tragic poets Verlaine and Rimbaud before them. So now you can be a poet and a businessman all at once. In fact, my mission in this book is to recast business as a romantic occupation. Coffee-shop nomads say that the noise and the chat are actually good for their concentration, and that you can see your target market all around you and study their habits.

So be free, be a boulevardier, be a *flâneur* with a laptop!

Afternoons for me are for meetings and looking after business, and evenings are for events, family and fun. It is that simple: philosophy, followed by husbandry, followed by merriment. The PHM system. Philosophy is the search for the good life, study, writing, reading, thinking;

husbandry is looking after ourselves, doing the accounts, managing our business, making bread, tending our garden; and merriment is health-giving laughter, dancing, singing and music-making – and drinking large quantities of high-quality beer, of course. In the middle of the twentieth century we delegated our merry-making to the professionals who entertain and distract us via the television. They do a very good job of it. But we should create more of our own fun – even if the fun we make is of admittedly lower quality than the expensively produced fun on the telly. Fun is therapeutic; it gives life purpose.

Time for Play

John Cleese said, 'If you want creative workers, make time for play.' That idea has the whiff of exploitation about it, as if you're tricking your staff into being productive, but it is, essentially, true. Good ideas emerge from doing nothing and mucking about. I am not personally a fan of the modern cult for putting a ping-pong table or table football in one corner of the office. This seems to be at best horrifically self-conscious, and at worst manipulative: a happy worker is a productive worker! Some of these modern workplaces do resemble cults, and I once worked for a cult-leader type. He constantly told us how amazing we were, how we were the best and how everyone else (every other magazine and department in our office) were idiots.

I suppose borrowing from cult-leader techniques is a management style and can work. I don't like it myself because it has the aura of the Brave New World about it. If you speak out as a cult member, then you will be accused of having a negative attitude and may be sent off for reprogramming.

On an individual level, then, you should find your own rhythm and your own way of slowing down and taking time out. You can encourage that culture among your staff as well, without imposing downtime as a duty.

Be a Flâneur

You have probably heard of the *flâneurs*. They were the disaffected poets of the late nineteenth century, the terminally gloomy Baudelaire and later jokers like the poet Gérard de Nerval. They took lobsters and tortoises for walks in order to slow their pace. They loved to amble through the city, watching and observing, not taking part, but always drinking in the sights, absorbing them, digesting them, fermenting them in their imaginations in the service of art.

You can do the same thing as a bohemian entrepreneur. Take frequent walks through the city. Wander round the supermarket. See what people are doing, how they behave, what they look like. Look at the busy shops and the quiet shops. Why do some places attract interest while others are ignored? The *flâneurs* would process whatever they saw into poetry and art. For you, whatever you see is free commercial information, and will be swilled around in that free business asset you have, your brain.

And while you are looking at what is going on and

processing it, try to get it clear in your mind exactly why you want to run your own business. Is it because you are a creative person and a freedom-seeker? If you are reading this, I imagine that money-making is not your top priority, and nor should it be. As my favourite management guru, Charles Handy, writes, making money is far from liberating: 'The individual pursuit of more money is a particular snare, because there is no obvious end to it. There will always be someone with more to act as a comparison and a challenge.'

Your business is a way of communicating an idea and creating a living for a group of people. It is a shared endeavour, a collective enterprise. Therefore, it must provide freedom and fun for the people you work with, as well as for you. After all, what is the point of it? If you just want to make money, then don't start a business. Go and work for some awful money-making machine and wallow in your own amoral wretchedness. Join a corporation, climb the ladder and enjoy paid holidays and multiple departments.

A business, says Charles Handy, should be a fun club. 'Is it not time to return to the idea of a business as a responsible community that pays heed to all its constituents, one whose core purpose must be to seek immortality through continuous self-improvement and investment? It is not a creation of shareholders, creditors and directors but an association of all those working in and with it. It is a community, a collection of people working together for a common purpose.'

Now, this bohemian ideal of a mutual association

working together to improve the lot of mankind might sometimes seem unachievable. And if that is the case, then remember that when the going gets tough, the tough will often take a nap, go for a long walk or otherwise indulge themselves in pure laziness . . . the advantages of which I outline in the next chapter.

15. The Power of Laziness

Put on with speed your woodland dress; / And bring no
book: for this one day / We'll give to idleness.
— Wordsworth

Now this, as Jerome K. Jerome once quipped, is a subject on which I consider myself to be fairly au fait. I have been researching idleness in its various forms for many years, at least since I was about eight, an angry, lazy, hot-headed and free-spirited boy.

In general, Western economies, like Germany, have the wrong-headed idea that every problem must be solved with more hard work, and that if the problem is not solved, then more hard work is required.

This approach, which was born in that grimmest of puritanical centuries, the sixteenth, is clearly absurd, since there is a limit to how hard one person can work. And hard workers do regularly reach that limit. An inbuilt defence system called 'the nervous breakdown' is the method the body uses to send a clear message to itself that something has gone very wrong indeed.

Hard work is only for the stupid, and this is as true in business as in everyday life. In fact, it is even more true in business, as the much-quoted and faintly irritating aphorism

'If you're working *in* your business, you're not working *on* your business' suggests. Laziness, indeed, leads directly to efficiency. Doing nothing solves problems. And you must preserve time to be creative.

There is a well-known poster which people put on their walls that says, 'Work hard and be nice to people.' That is terrible business advice. If you work hard and are nice to people, you will end up working sixteen hours a day while people swan off with your money. Better advice would be: 'Be lazy and be a complete bastard.'

In one single week not long ago I read two articles in the papers which argued that laziness is a business asset. Why? Because lazy people find the clever way to do things. They do not overwork, so their heads are clearer. I certainly do not demand that my staff kill themselves. And nor do they. Julian leaves on the dot of six every day. That is good; he is efficient. And Bobbie works from wherever she happens to be with her laptop. That is good, too, as she catches up at odd moments through the week.

The first piece, in the *Daily Telegraph*, featured the appealing headline 'Why being Lazy and Procrastinating Could Make You Wildly Successful'. In a paragraph entitled 'You can only be lazy if you're clever', the piece offered the thoughts of a pre-war Prussian Army general:

> Kurt von Hammerstein-Equord was Germany's chief of the army before the Second World War. He supposedly said that all his officers were two of the following: clever, diligent, stupid or lazy. According to the general, the most dangerous officer was one who was stupid and

diligent. He couldn't be trusted with any responsibility because he would always make mischief.

However, officers who were both clever and lazy were qualified for the highest leadership duties, because they possessed the intellectual clarity and the 'composure' necessary for difficult decisions.

They are masters at avoiding 'busywork' such as pointless meetings, he claimed, they delegate to others to get things done efficiently, and they focus on the essentials rather than being distracted by unnecessary extras.

The same argument was advanced by *Financial Times* columnist Lucy Kellaway. She told the story of a friend who had cut down her work hours as a result of spending a lot of time with a new boyfriend. The effect on her career had been positive because she had learned to become more efficient.

Kellaway ponders:

This experience has led her to a new theory of success that says laziness is good. It is only by being lazy that we become truly efficient, and come to see what is important and what is not. The trouble with women, she went on, is that we try too hard. We make ourselves martyrs to industriousness, and far from that being our secret advantage, it is our undoing. If only we were lazier, we would do better.

It is wrongly said that Bill Gates employs lazy people because they get the work done more efficiently. However, this theory was indeed advanced by an efficiency expert called Frank B. Gilbreth Senior, who observed the relative efficiency of groups of bricklayers. A 1920 piece for a magazine called *Popular Science Monthly* reported:

> Gilbreth studied the methods of various bricklayers – the poor workmen and the best ones, and he stumbled upon an astonishing fact of great importance and significance. He found that he could learn most from the lazy man!
>
> Most of the chance improvements in human motions that eliminate unnecessary movement and reduce fatigue have been hit upon, Gilbreth thinks, by men who were lazy – so lazy that every needless step counted.

In the same way, the Taoist butcher finds the easiest path through the meat with his knife. The longer you work at something, the more easily you are able to do it.

The best way is the easiest way – but, paradoxically, it may take a lot of work to find it.

Gilbreth invented a unit of energy called the 'Therblig' (his name backwards, almost), and his children, also management theorists, explained that the instinct to conserve and not waste Therbligs was demonstrated by the lazy man. Therefore, laziness – in the sense of not wasting energy – leads to efficiency. The Gilbreth kids wrote in a 1948 management manual of their own: 'A lazy man, Dad believed, always makes the best use of his Therbligs because he is too indolent to waste motions. Whenever Dad started to do a new motion study project at a factory, he'd always begin by announcing he wanted to photo-graph the motions of the laziest man on the job.'

I understand that the financier Jim Slater always took Fridays off. His staff knew that he could not be contacted on that day.

In my own case, my ability to write at high speed comes from a desire to get the work out of the way as quickly as possible so I can go down the pub. It was the same with Dr Johnson: he thought for many hours before starting a piece of writing. That looked like indolence. Then he would write at great speed before going down to the tav-ern with Topham Beauclerk, Bennet Langton and the other young dogs of London town.

These days, I take the odd Friday off and go for a long walk around London with an old friend.

Against Plodding

No one likes a plodder. They make you feel bad. They are impolite. They squander their Therbligs in the hope of being seen to be a hard-working, diligent little slave-worker by the slave manager. I remember working in an office many years ago. One of my colleagues was a sour-faced gentleman who never seemed to leave the office. How-ever early I arrived, however late I left, there he was, sullenly staring at his computer, working hard.

His surly presence created a huge downer in the office. He was like a black hole, sucking all the energy out of the place. Presumably, he thought that by sitting at his desk 24/7, he was reducing his chances of being sacked. In fact, he just came across as a total pain in the neck, and my life improved immeasurably when I quit that job.

Either love it, or quit it. Don't sit there in a state of seething resentment, moaning to everyone around you, making their lives miserable.

Now, I am not saying that being late is cool, far from it. I think that we responsible bohemians, once we have made an agreement, should stick to it. (By the way, arriving ten minutes early to a meeting gives you extra idle time: walk around the block, sit on a bench, do nothing.)

And I am not saying that staff should sit around doing nothing, merely conserving their Therbligs. I realize now that calling a shop the Idler Academy was an invitation to loaf. What I could not understand was that the staff seemed to have no initiative and didn't bother tidying, cleaning and dreaming up ways to sell more books when we weren't there. Instead, they checked their phones and social-media networks.

As I mentioned, I wrote a sign which read 'No idling' and put it up in the kitchen at work. It had no effect. 'It's the customers who should be idling!' I shouted at our loafing helpers. 'Not the staff!' Inefficient, chaotic and ostentatiously 'laid-back' staff make for a stressful experience for the punter.

One great business bohemian friend of mine is John Mitchinson. He is a true free spirit, with a gigantic laugh, a huge beard and a massively positive attitude to life. But he takes on too much. We were hanging out in Brighton after an event and I asked him how everything was going. 'Oh God, you know, two jobs,' he said, with a note of despair. His two jobs at that point were writing all the books for *QI* and being co-founder of Unbound, the crowdfunding book publisher. Both great jobs. But very demanding. And then he said loudly, as if trying to convince himself: 'We do it because we love it!'

'We do it because we love it': that is the mantra of the business bohemian. Because, if we didn't love it, what would be the point of all the suffering?

Idling and Efficiency

Idling is good in three ways: it is enjoyable in itself; it is good for the health; and it is creatively fertile. Idling is therefore a business asset not only because you will not be tired all the time but because it is when we are idle that we start thinking. But we need to be efficient in order to be idle. We need to make time for idling, and we need to be pretty ruthless about it.

So how can we be efficient? It is not easy, particularly if, like me, you have a tendency to revert to a state of chaos if given half the chance. Also, other people are quite happy to bust into your idle time. You have to be very strict with them.

The therapist and author Rachel Kelly says that her trick is to ensure that the hour from two till three every day is her quiet time. That is when she shuts the door and reads, rests, snoozes or meditates, and no one is allowed to interrupt her. If she misses her hour off, she says, her whole day collapses. If you want to be idle, you have to learn how to shut the door.

You also have to learn how to turn off the phone and any other electronic devices. The idea that you should always be available or in touch is for the slaves. The problem with the phone – as well as its supposed advantage – is that it enables you to work anywhere. I remember thinking while walking through London to a meeting as I checked my emails, 'Wow, this is amazing. I can now work while walking.' I fooled myself into thinking that it was a good idea to be constantly checking emails, as it meant that I would be faced with less work when I sat down with my laptop.

Recently, however, by accident, I dropped my phone in the loo. The phone-free weeks which followed have shown me that four hours on the laptop in the morning and a couple spread out over the afternoon and evening is enough to keep on top of emails. I have zero unchecked emails in my inbox.

I also found that the emails I composed on my phone were brief and hasty, to the point of being rude. I would argue that being smartphone-free leads to a higher level of courtesy. So, if you crave more headspace in your every-day life, I recommend swapping your smartphone for a dumb-phone.

Do you have any other useless addictions you could quit? The actress Emma Thompson, esteemed patron of the Idler Academy, and her husband, Greg Wise, never (or very rarely) read newspapers or watch television. This helps them to remain unstressed. The news is particularly addictive and troubling. However, you may feel that you want to know what is going on in the world. I like to be tolerably well-informed, and I have reduced my newspaper habit to reading the *International New York Times*, which is about a million times superior to any of the Brit papers.

The Need to Get Away

I am not a big fan of holidays, because they are horrifically expensive and, anyway, I don't have a life that I want to get away from. For me, every day is a holiday, in a sense. Bohemians do not crave holidays in the same way as wage slaves.

However, I appreciate that we all benefit from a change of scene, and from exposure to the countryside, a river, the sun or the sea. So I do think that it is wise in our every-day life to arrange some sort of dacha system, a little retreat for yourself. I don't mean that you have to buy a holiday cottage. That is just another burden. But could you share the cost of a canal boat with another family, or rent a field and put a caravan on it? Could you frequent a particular campsite?

Without such resources to hand, my own trick, now that I am back in the city, is to find a park bench to escape to. Park benches are a wonderful and under-used resource for idling, reading, thinking and dozing.

Read Real Books

If I have a good book on the go, I look forward to going to bed. This helps stop me from drinking too much. And gets me to bed early. Reading a good book – a real book, not an ebook, which are so full of problems I'm not even going to talk about it – offers an escape from the screen and feeds your mind and soul with good ingredients. In the same way that we are all aware of healthy food, we should be aware of healthy books. I might even invent some kind of health-ranking system for books. In the same way that the world of restaurants has its Slow Food movement, should we introduce a Slow Reading movement that recommends healthy, nutritious reading material?

Work Smart

In the States, the will towards doing as little as possible has been renamed 'work smart'. This means that instead of sitting at a desk and working sixteen hours a day, you should be efficient. There's a chap called Ari Meisel, an 'efficiency guru', who is the Frank B. Gilbreth Senior of our day. He has been called 'the most efficient man alive'. With his shaved head and shapeless grey tops, Ari looks more like a DHL delivery man than a guru. He travels around the States giving talks which help people to 'get better at what they do'. His technique is to recommend a load of websites and apps which are supposed to help you get organized.

'Efficiency is my passion,' says Ari. His website is called lessdoing.org, and boasts the following slogan: 'Less Doing, More Living: Make Everything in Life Easier.' It features video footage of a group of T-shirted men staring at laptops, becoming efficient, being positive. One of the laptops bears the slightly over-positive legend 'I can, I will.'

By all means, check it out. I did. Ari's trick for freeing you from technology is to recommend a long list of 'productivity' websites, things like Evernote and iDoneThis. These self-regarding start-ups are supposed to make you into some sort of super-human cyborg who starts up billion-dollar companies while spending hours of quality time with your three-year-old son – and makes your own granola.

Ari's mantra is 'Outsource, optimize, automate' and, on the surface, this injunction might seem to be an attractive option for bohemians. After all, it would be nice if we had a butler, a manservant or a secretary to do the menial stuff while we dozed in a hammock reading Shelley. If that manservant is a piece of technology, then great.

I do accept that scheduling is an excellent idea. Website systems like WordPress enable you to schedule an article or new product release: your website will update itself while you are dozing on the roof of a canal boat a hundred miles outside the city. You can also schedule tweets. That seems like a good idea. Schedule ten tweets a day and, again, you can go for a nap while the computer gets on with it.

However, I think that, in general, if you are suffering from a surfeit of technology, then do not ask technology to solve that problem for you. Just leave your phone at home and go for a walk. Tell your friends and associates that you may not have a phone signal. I remember taking my phone with me on a rowing trip down the Thames. My brother and I had taken our daughters on a Lewis Carroll tribute trip and rented a rowboat. As we blissfully picnicked on the side of the Cherwell at Christchurch Meadow, dreaming of white rabbits, my phone beeped. There was a new tweet. Oh, that's nice, I thought. And clicked on it. Here's what it said: '@idleracademy Why do you persist with absurd bad grammar award? Have you no shame?'

Oh dear, it was a trolling tweet from our enemy, a hack called Oliver Kamm, a leader writer on *The Times*, who had taken against our annual Bad Grammar Award, through which we attempt to expose bullshit in the written word. He – wrongly – believed the award to be a reactionary, elitist idea. I felt a sort of nervous sensation emerge in my stomach and throat. I suppose I should be more thick-skinned, but the unpleasant tweet from Mr Kamm quite ruined the moment. Clearly, I would have had a much better day if I'd had a dumb-phone, or simply no phone at all. Why on earth had I left it on? It was a Saturday, on a meadow, by a river, in Oxford, with my daughter, in spring. Pure madness.

The whole point of being a bohemian in business is to escape slavery. If you end up becoming your own jailer, then something has gone wrong. Try to avoid the temptation to build a cage for yourself, however comfortably furnished that cage might be.

A few doors down from our shop is one run by an

antique dealer. She rents her shop, fills it with beautiful stuff, and the place doubles as office and gallery. She is her own boss. What's not to like? 'I'm living in a padded cell!' she complained to me one day. She had created a wonderful space but never seemed to leave it. So her New Year's resolution was to get out more.

So, when the going gets tough, do as little as possible. Be lazy. Take long walks. Nap. Sleep a lot. Read books. This way, you will not only feel in control of your life, you will improve the lives of the people around you, and you will improve your business, too.

The way forward is hard. There will be many obstacles. You will need to be tough and to develop the right attitude, a kind of Zen-like stoicism, and that is the subject of our next chapter.

16. How to be Stoic

Nothing is so bitter that a calm mind cannot find comfort in it.

– Seneca the Younger

In ancient Athens, two rival schools of philosophy sprang up. One was an attitude to life pioneered by the guru Epicurus, who was born in 341BC. He said that in order to be happy and fulfilled, you should get out of the city and escape its vanities and temptations. Instead, you should live with a group of others on a farm, be self-sufficient, reduce your needs and cultivate simplicity. He was a sort of proto-Gandhi figure.

The other group was called the Stoics. Its founder, Zeno of Citium, born in 334BC, reckoned, contrariwise, that the best thing was to put up with the slings and arrows that outrageous fortune seems to make a habit of hurling at us 24/7 and create coping mechanisms.

I've tried both philosophical approaches. I retired from the city in 2002 and lived in a farmhouse for twelve years. There I lived the Epicurean life. I wrote five books there and brought up my children. I grew vegetables. That worked fine. But when I opened a shop and a small business and became a petit-bourgeois, the Epicurean life collapsed, as I simply did not have the energy to grow vegetables any more. I was thrown into a new world of anxiety, debt and worry, the world of the shopkeeper and small-business owner, the fledgling merchant. Getting away from it all was not an option: we had signed a five-year lease on a shop and taken out a loan that was to be paid back over five years. There was no escape. In this case, Stoicism, not Epicureanism, was the correct philosophy.

We'll go into that in a moment. But why would you need to think about philosophy when starting a business? Surely philosophy is a subject to be studied at university? Something to do with the non-existence of matter?

Philosophy in its original sense meant 'love of wisdom', and it was a kind of religious study for the ancient Greeks. It concerned itself with the very practical question of how to live the good life. And they debated endlessly about how this could be achieved.

I am urging you to learn about the Stoics because, as a bohemian in business, you will face enormous hurdles and problems, daily, and the Stoic philosophy is the answer. It will help you to be tough without turning into a complete bastard. It will help you to develop the emotional and spiritual tools that you will need to cope. Every entrepreneur has a long list of failures, setbacks, disasters and nightmares behind (and ahead of) them. This book indeed is, in part, a catalogue of all the headaches that Victoria and I had to cope with during our first five years of running a business.

There is a trait which is common to people who have attempted to go down the path of launching their own business, and that is to 'catastrophize'. Many times over the years, I have been heard to shout, 'What's the point?' 'What are we going to do?' 'I give up! I can't face this any more!'

I never do give up, though. Again, it's back to that same piece of advice: 'Just . . . keep . . . going.' That, I think, is Stoicism in practice.

I often lose my temper, and my outbursts can make life pretty horrific for the people I live with. So it would behoove the individual to develop a reasonably cheerful attitude and make a daily practice of remaining open-minded and humble. These days, you are supposed to be full of self-esteem, but that quality, to me, can veer dangerously close to pride, a sin. 'Beware pride' seems to be a central tenet in the Stoic approach.

The first step, I think, is not to be too hard on yourself for exploding. Luke Johnson reckons that the ups and downs of being an entrepreneur are part and parcel of the whole thing. You have to live with it. He says he prefers that sort of drama – heaven and hell – to the purgatorial tedium of being a posh slave in the office.

Who were the Stoics?

Sometimes thought of as a precursor to the Christians, the Stoics were like the Taoists of the ancient Western world. They attempted to remain unruffled in the face of adversity. Zeno of Citium was the bored son of a merchant and had a taste for philosophy. The story goes that he was in Athens on a bit of shore leave while helping out his father. He wandered into a bookshop and started reading a book by Xenophon, the Greek soldier who recorded Socrates' dialogues. A wild-haired character called Crates wandered past the shop. The bookseller told Zeno that this was Crates the Cynic, a follower of Socrates. The Cynics were bohemians, punks, free spirits: they scorned convention, wore ripped clothes, refused to work, lived in barrels, masturbated in public, gatecrashed parties and generally didn't care about anything. And they made a big show of not caring as well. Think Johnny Rotten.

Zeno followed Crates and then adapted the Cynical philosophy into something more practical. The Stoics were not concerned with rejecting convention. To do that was itself another convention. They believed that life is grounded in what they called the *logos*, similar to what the Taoists called the Tao, or the Way. It can be translated as 'the word', 'the way', or even 'the joke'. Attune yourself with the *logos* and you will be OK. Things go wrong in life when you resist its flow. The Stoics chose not to escape the city but to live in it. They taught in a part of the marketplace called the *stoa*, hence their name.

The Stoics taught that you should 'go with the flow'. They believed in fate. Life is like a cylinder rolling down a hill. As *Idler* friend Mark Vernon puts it in his guide to ancient philosophy, 'Your freedom lies in embracing the knocks and the blows, trusting that all will end well in the valley. Suffering arises from hating and bemoaning and cursing and fearing the knocks and blows.'

Well, ain't that the truth! Though to bear the blows with equanimity is a very difficult task indeed, as we all know.

The Stoics had a number of tricks to help you with this. First, they taught that you should first train yourself to rise above petty anger when it came to the small things. Someone jumps the queue at the olive stall? Hey, don't sweat it. Be benignly indifferent.

Train yourself to cope with little adversities and you will gradually grow able to cope with larger ones. The Stoic philosophy has been hugely successful. The Romans took it up with gusto. Marcus Aurelius was the first Stoic emperor, about four hundred and fifty years after the movement was founded. It was hugely influential on the development of early Christianity as well. Think about the Stoicism that Christ displayed.

One common misinterpretation of Stoicism is that it's all about cultivating a 'stiff upper lip' and repressing emotion. Though I am not a fan of the theories of Mr Freud, it is surely true that repressed feelings can fester in the mind and the soul and do damage. Stoicism, however, is a joyful surrender to the river of life and means taking control of your emotions rather than being controlled by them. However, you should also listen to your emotions. The modern version of this is called Cognitive Behavioural Therapy, an ugly new name for a beautiful old concept. The central difference with CBT is that it does not ask you to believe in the *logos*.

What has this got to do with business? Well, as our locksmith said, 'Business is a spiritual thing.' It is going to throw a huge number of tests and trials in your path. You will not be able to hide behind a boss or a parent. This process will help you to become a stronger person, happier, more fulfilled, more in control, more humble, whatever happens, whether you succeed or fail. As I've mentioned before, it is not about hard work and it is not about money. It is about freedom and taking responsibility for yourself.

Within the corporate world, CEOs and top executives are surrounded by a battery of people who help them. Such is their self-importance – or their perceived importance to the company – that they have their own personal task force of therapists, life coaches, chauffeurs, personal trainers, concierge services, PAs and mindfulness gurus. They are like babies. You, as a wild-haired bohemian, do not have this luxury. You are on your own. At least at the beginning, you will be doing everything. And that is better. Because when the pampered CEO is torn from the protective bosom of Mummy, what will they do? They will start to cry.

You are strong, fearless, self-sufficient, you make time for reading, thinking, quiet contemplation, meditation or prayer. This need not cost a penny. The world is full of beautiful churches which were built with the express intention of lifting and calming the spirit, and you can wander into one at lunchtime wherever you are and grab some peace. You can meditate on a park bench. And you could read the central Stoic texts, such as Seneca's

Dialogues and *Letters* and *The Handbook* by Epictetus. Keep them by your bedside and dip in.

Grow Fond of Failure

Fifty per cent of new businesses fail. That is a lot. You have only a fifty-fifty chance of making it into your fourth year. We are now entering our fifth year and, though I cannot claim to have made a million pounds, or anything like that, we have certainly succeeded in our aims of creating a great school, selling books, having fun and meeting interesting people. We have turned over a million quid thus far, but we've also paid out over £125,000 in rent and over £150,000 in wages, to say nothing of the fees we've paid our tutors.

However, I am not angry about the situation we're in, because it has been created by me and Victoria. Nobody else. Therefore, I cannot complain. If I want to make a bigger profit, I will have to sit down and cut costs and increase revenues. (Clearly, easier said than done.) And I am the one who has chosen to pay people to do the work rather than attempting to do everything myself.

When I think about the bigger picture, the high failure rate of new businesses, it looks like we're doing pretty well. However, if you do fail, then you should embrace failure as an opportunity to learn. Your business is something separate from you; it is not you. And if you associate yourself too closely with it, you will go mad.

This, I think, is a Stoic trick that can help you to keep

your head while all around you people are losing theirs. Enjoy failure on a small scale. In the beginning, I was horrified by things going wrong. And I felt overwhelmed by being the go-to guy for every issue, from televisions not working, to VAT returns, to asbestos reports, to raising money. Yet again, I would rant to Victoria, 'Why does everyone come straight to me for every tiny problem?'

Then I started to carry a little notebook with me which I called 'The Wrong Book'. Each day, I would open up our shop and assume that everything would go wrong. Instead of panicking, I would simply write down whatever it was that went wrong in my book. Examples might be: books out of order on the shelves; tables dusty; Tarquin late; tea urn left on; kitchen messy; details for evening event not on Google Drive; VAT return late. And so on. In each case, we needed to develop a little system that dealt with the issue. Things going wrong should be fun; it is how you learn. In the early days, in particular, you lurch from crisis to crisis, and that is to be expected.

Things going wrong teach you to remain humble. If everything always went right, Aristotle said, what sort of an unpleasant person would you turn into? Failure wards off complacency, which is an enemy, in business and in life.

As the Stoics taught, if you learn to enjoy the small failures and disasters, you will be better placed to cope with the big failures and disasters when they, inevitably, come. Every failure teaches you an enormous amount. You should start by training yourself not to lose your temper over trivial issues, such as leaving your mobile phone at home. Then you will be able, over time, to cope with bigger and bigger problems.

Author and teacher Jules Evans has made a business out of his love for philosophy. He writes books, runs courses, organizes conferences and works as the in-house philosopher at Saracens rugby club. For him, the Stoic attitude is one of the best ways to approach the unavoidable ups and downs that accompany his life of freedom. He says, 'Stoicism is a philosophy of self-reliance, and that's particularly useful for entrepreneurs, who have to cope with failure and the fear of failure, uncertainty, status volatility, and other obstacles. Finding the right mindset to deal with these obstacles is crucial, and a lot of entrepreneurs have found Stoicism to be the best "operating system", as Tim Ferriss [author of *The 4-hour Work Week*] puts it.' Adds Stoic philosopher Jules Evans, 'Of course, you can overdo self-reliance – it's also useful to share your suffering with others rather than just bottling it up.'

The Bohemian Wobble

I read something by a Silicon Valley start-up guru who said that the worst that can happen if your business fails is that you will have to get a job. So it can't be that bad.

I try to make a point of counting my blessings each morning. I am free. I do not have to go to a job I hate. I know both from memory, and from friends now who are stuck in boring jobs, that all the money in the world could not compensate me for the loss of freedom they entail.

That is, however, not to say that I have not suffered from what I call the 'bohemian wobble'. This is some variant of the following thought process: 'What's the point? I am working my butt off and I have no money. Worse, I am actually in debt. I can't afford to go on holiday. (OK, I don't approve of them in principle but, once in a while, it might be nice to get away.) I am denying cereals to my children. I am in a constant state of fury. I went down the wrong path when I rejected conventional employment twenty-five years ago. If I'd gone into nursing, I'd be earning more than I do now. To say nothing of being a dentist, or a doctor, or an orthodontist. Bohemianism doesn't work. Even the successful ones go mad. Look at Amy Winehouse. I should have trained as a chartered accountant.'

The System seems expressly invented to make you, as a bohemian, fail and to encourage conformity. The sensible thing would be for both partners in a relationship to train as dentists, then use their enormous salaries to secure enormous mortgages and buy loads of flats and houses which they then rent out. Laughing! Don't write books, paint pictures, start magazines, teach grammar or open bookshops. That way lies penury and toil. Hark my words: become a healthcare professional, and you actually get paid.

I have seen this phenomenon occur in loads of my creative friends, those brave individuals who reckoned they could make a living out of their creativity, rather than just getting on with it and going to work for a bank, a corporate giant or the civil service. They find themselves in middle age worrying about money. The income of the creative classes has been reduced enormously over the last twenty years because Internet companies now provide so much art and culture for free. One journalist friend, a very successful former editor of *Cosmopolitan*, reckons that she is earning one eighth, in real terms, of what she earned twenty years ago.

So a full-time job with its paid holidays and no need to do VAT and tax returns can occasionally look very attractive to the harried small-business owner. When we were setting up our shop, we went to visit a café on Exmoor which was closing down, with an eye to buying their chairs. The owners, a couple approaching retirement age, were completely fed up. 'All I want is a part-time job I don't have to think about,' said the male half. 'Maybe in a DIY superstore. Turn up, go home, get paid, don't worry.'

And some bohemians find that conventional jobs work well for them. There was a great eighties punk band called Big Black, led by American musician and producer Steve Albini. He loved having a job: he worked as a photo-retoucher when he was starting out in bands. It gave him income and holidays, and he left his work behind in the office. That meant he could play in bands without worrying overmuch about making a living from it. He would go on tour during his paid holidays.

Now, if you find that you are overcome by the bohemian wobble or get an attack of what's-the-pointness, first, remind yourself of your own superiority to all the slaves out there, even the well-paid ones. Remember Luke Johnson's comment about his lawyer and banker mates: 'It's just posh slavery.'

You can also think, Well, I don't have to do this for ever. In fact, if we chose to, we could liquidate the business and do something else. Businesses go bust every day, and there is no shame in it. You may decide that the business world is not for you. One friend, who has been in the commercial world for many years, is retraining as a teacher. He is fed up, he says, with the childish idiots he meets in business, so has decided he'd rather work with children.

I think the point is: you don't *have* to do this. If you don't like it, you should give up. But if you keep going, there is the chance that you could earn some real money and create something that will last for many years, will spread a message around the world, employ people, and provide you with meaning and money.

There is little money in journalism. Even a very successful journalist would be lucky to earn much more than a bricklayer – and certainly they'd earn less than a plumber. So I decided to start up a new enterprise with the hope of creating an entity that will outlive me, improve people's lives and provide satisfying work for a lot of people, including my children, if they are interested. Not an easy task, but a noble one, I think!

The Importance of Plan B

Over the years, I have learned always, when going for a particular objective, to formulate a Plan B that you would be perfectly happy with. For example, what would happen if we did not achieve our crowdfunding target? Well, we would just carry on in a small way, and grow organically. We might have to cut back a bit on staff – and I warned Bobbie and Julian that this might happen.

On another occasion, a well-known speaker was threatening to pull out of giving a talk on one of our courses. So I lined up a replacement in case this actually happened. Then I went back to her and asked if she would consider not cancelling. Because I didn't care about the outcome, I was in a strong negotiating position. And she did the talk.

As I mentioned in our chapter on negotiation, the key is not to get too attached to one particular outcome. For, that way, madness lies.

The Joy of Small

A phrase I hear often among creative small-business owners is 'It's a nightmare, but it's my nightmare.' These words encapsulate the paradox of the whole thing: it is better to be trapped in a nightmare of your own creation than to be trapped in a nightmare of someone else's creation. This is the result of freedom. It may be hard. But it is vastly preferable to slavery.

17. The Joys of Quitting

O, for an age so sheltered from annoy,
That I may never know how change the moons
Or hear the voice of busy common-sense!

— Keats, 'Ode on Indolence'

At one of my 'reality check' meetings with John Brown, he took a piece of paper out of a drawer and read out to me his top-ten tips for aspiring entrepreneurs. When it came to point ten, he lifted up the piece of paper, shoved it in my face and jabbed his finger at the writing. I leaned in to read it: 'Know when to give up.'

Thanks for the vote of confidence, John.

But he is right: quitting at the right time, or knowing when to abandon a certain product or project, is an important skill.

In 2016, having run it for five years, we gave up our first retail outlet. We decided not to renew the lease on our outpost in Notting Hill. The shop had worked for us brilliantly as a base, office, venue, shop and marketing trick, but the overheads were growing too high for what we were getting out of it. We decided it would be sensible to reduce our overheads and use other people's venues for the time being. Let them worry about landlords. We'll send them people.

A note: if you are planning to open a shop, think about it seriously first. There are many snares for the unwary. Firstly, the set-up costs are huge: we had to pay £3,000 to a solicitor; a £9,000 deposit to the landlord; £5,000 to the book wholesaler for stock; and £20,000 to the shop-fitters. Then, when we left the premises, we had to spend £6,000 of the deposit redecorating and in fees to the landlord's surveyor! The terms of the leases are very much in the landlord's favour.

During our first three years or so of being at the cutting edge of retail, we gave up many of our most dearly cherished ideas. Originally, we had wanted to serve breakfast and lunch as well as run events and courses every evening. Only as time wore on did we realize that this was completely insane and that we had taken on far too much: bookshop, publisher, organic café, live-events venue, meeting place, office, club, retreat, media brand, live-events consulting firm, pop-ups all over London and at festivals . . . I was in danger of damaging my 'idler' credentials.

Live the brand, Tom! Don't overwork!

At the start, I became obsessed by cafés and read a series of books on how to create a successful coffee shop. It all seemed like a lot of hard work. Soy milk: should you offer it, or not? Indeed, some customers would primly enquire if we had soy milk. Instead of just saying no, I would sneak to the newsagent's, spend two quid on a carton of the stuff and completely destroy our profit margin on that particular cup of coffee.

Our service was way too slow. I remember once, when an illustrious American historian came in. I'd met him before at a restaurant when I'd been a full-time writer and he'd been charming. Now he seemed quite grumpy. He didn't recognize me. He ordered a coffee, which Damson went downstairs to make, and browsed our book selection. 'They've got the complete works of Aristotle,' he said to his friend, impressed. But then, after a few minutes, he swung around to me and said, 'Am I going to have to go down there and make this coffee myself?'

We never saw him again. It was the same with Brett Anderson from Suede. I think he had to wait half an hour for his coffee. My son Arthur was helping us, and he was eleven at the time. He dropped the coffee on the stairs and we had to start again. 'Where the fuck is this coffee?' I hissed at Victoria in the kitchen. She was so appalled by my behaviour she stormed out, leaving me to apologize to Brett. He was very nice about it, but he never came back.

Friends who had absolutely no idea what they were talking about suddenly became experts on coffee shops, for example, 'Open at 8 a.m. and you'll clean up with yummy mummies.' My brother, who has a full-time job and has never been anywhere near a small business, would say things like, 'The thing you have to understand about running your own business is . . . [insert platitude here].' Customers would come in and ask about what sort of coffee we sold. I would patiently explain that we did Monmouth coffee, from single-estate farms in Brazil, freshly ground, slow-roasted, using a pour-over filter system.

'That's OK, I'll leave it. I'm pretty fussy about my coffee,' they would say.

Every morning at five thirty I would wake up and start worrying. 'Systems, systems, *we need a system!*' I would shout at Victoria. Later, Bobbie and Julian helped us to create great systems that really worked. I tried, but, somehow, in the middle of the firefighting, I didn't seem to be able to find the time to sit down and work out an opening routine, a closing routine and all the rest of it. Instead, I'd be cleaning the loo in a panic while plucking up the courage to ask the intern to hoover the basement at 6.30 p.m., just as the great and good of Notting Hill were arriving for a talk on the Reform Bill of 1832 by Lady Antonia Fraser.

I would stare forlornly through the windows of Starbucks and wonder why their queues were so long when our café was so much nicer. Probably something to do with their systems. They probably have whole departments of Yale graduates working on their systems, brilliant geeks, constantly refining Starbucks' offerings. They probably employ the world's top psychologists to work out which colours make people spend more money. Not to mention huge other teams working on buying coffee for practically nothing. I developed a new respect for McDonald's. There was something beautiful about their system, a system which could be replicated all over the world.

I would sit all day in our empty café and bookshop, and when working the occasional Saturday would stare at the huge crowds outside the pub opposite. I don't think any one of that pub's customers ever came into our shop to buy a book. I would be delighted when I saw the shambling figure of Peter, a disturbed local who sometimes sat in the corner bellowing about being stuck in the wrong version of reality, approach the shop. At least he would buy a couple of coffees, even if he did scare off the other customers by accusing them of stealing his soul.

At other times, I would see someone approaching the shop and get excited for a moment, wondering if we had a real customer. Then they would glance at the window, take a photograph, which they probably put on Instagram, and then go to the pub to spend some money. Or someone would come in and ask, 'Do you know the way to Portobello Road?'

Running a small café was pretty hopeless. I would go to the supermarket in the morning and buy three croissants. They would sit on the counter all morning, and then we'd eat them for lunch. I tried to do the best ever ploughman's lunch, which we called the Idle Ploughman's Lunch. It came with an organic apple and a slice of organic pork pie from Legges of Herefordshire. We sold about two a week and ate the rest ourselves. We agonized over whether we should buy or rent a coffee machine. In the end – thank God – we decided against it. They cost thousands of pounds.

'Bookshops and restaurants – nice idea, but don't,' said Charles Handy to me the other day. In hindsight, it was a bit crazy of us to open a combined restaurant and bookshop in a very quiet corner of west London with no passing trade when we knew absolutely nothing about either.

Looking back, it was obvious that we were never going to make any money selling the occasional croissant and organic pork pie. In the end, we settled down with a great cake supplier plus a Nespresso machine in addition to our Monmouth pour-over thing and a few herbal teas. That was it: an urn and a counter. Easy.

Funnily enough, the bookshop side of things has worked quite well, and could work better if we were in a better location. And that is entirely due to Julian, who knows how to run an interesting bookshop with great efficiency. So maybe we'll open another little bookshop one day.

As I mentioned earlier, I also discovered in this process that I really enjoyed selling books. To me, it was like an extension of journalism. It was a piece of communication. I remember selling a young philosophy student a copy of Foucault's *History of Sexuality* and thinking, This is fun. To sell a pile of books that you have recommended to someone, and to know that they are going to go off and enjoy them, is a pleasurable experience.

Making a cup of coffee for someone, on the other hand, is hell and brought me out in a cold sweat almost every time. You have to give it your full concentration, and you are worried that the customer is not going to enjoy it. It's a nerve-racking business.

The point is, if something is not working out, because it is making you miserable, or you can't do it, or no one's buying what you're trying to sell, then stop and do something else.

What makes me happy is sitting down on my own writing or working on my own for four hours every morning.

It's that simple. The rest of the day, I'm happy to blob around in the shop, or sleep, or do accounts, or have meetings. The team we have now can do all the hard work. They're good at it, they enjoy it: let them do it.

So give up the things that make you unhappy.

It would be sensible to sit down and make a list of the things you enjoy and the things you hate. Look at the hate list. Can you cut some of those things out of your life completely, or delegate them to someone else? Victoria hates computers and numbers so we have asked other people to sort that stuff out for us.

Of course, this process takes time. Small-business owners often complain that they have to do absolutely everything, hence the entrepreneur's little joke, that CEO stands for Chief Everything Officer. You are chairman, cleaner, coffee maker, head of marketing, product-development manager – the whole shebang. Gradually, you will learn which of these roles you can pass to someone else – or, indeed, outsource or automate – and which you will continue to do yourself.

It's big-headed to think that you know best about everything. You need to be humble and to listen to people who have more experience in each zone of your business. Just because you have *been* to a café or a bookshop doesn't mean you know how to *run* a café or a bookshop.

Here is a list of twelve other things we gave up doing:

1. **Selling second-hand books.** In addition to running an independent bookshop, café, adult-education centre, lecture venue and community

hub, we also reckoned that we could add a second-hand bookshop into the mix. I would drive to a dealer on the A303, give him £200, walk out with a pile of books, and never sell them. Most of them are still sitting on the shelves four years later.

2. **Members' club.** We had the idea that all our friends would join our club membership scheme and come and hang out all day in our shop, quipping like Dorothy Parker at the Algonquin Round Table. It would be a non-stop salon, peopled by the wits of the day. In the end, only poet Murray Lachlan Young popped in regularly. We dropped the idea of a members' club.

3. **Art gallery.** We thought selling art would be easy. Just put a friend's canvas in the window, sell it for £500, keep half. It wasn't. A well-known footballer once enquired after our painting of Rupert the Bear by Mark Manning but didn't buy it. In the end, we took it home.

4. **Herb and lettuce garden.** At one point we had the idea of growing our own mint and lettuces in the garden. We dropped this one fairly swiftly.

5. **Selling books by local authors.** We were besieged by self-publicising, self-published local authors who suggested that we take twenty copies of their book. We would take one, and even that would turn out to be a mistake, as the author would keep popping in to see if anyone had bought their memoir about their grandmother. When we said

no, they would criticize the way we had displayed the book. One local author, a statuesque African woman with false eyelashes who called herself Nefertiti, brought in a copy of her hand-written book, a guide to the mysteries of the pyramids. When I said that we couldn't stock it, she put a curse on us. Maybe it worked: I don't know. I didn't see her for three years, until she turned up at a party we held for Youth, the laid-back music producer, where she drank some free beer and told the other guests that she'd put bad juju on us.

6. **Talking to customers.** OK, this was just me. In the early days, I was quite delighted when readers came in and told me how much they had enjoyed my books. They would then go on to tell me about their own life, how they could not get their spouse to read my books and how they were considering moving to a smallholding in Portugal. After about two hours of philosophical conversation, I would think, Hang on. Is this going anywhere? Are they going to buy a book? I learned to hide from customers.

7. **Selling books in Latin and Greek.** I am a fan of the Loeb editions of the ancient classics. They are dinky little hardbacks with the original Latin or Greek on the left and an English translation on the right. So I bought a dozen to sell in the shop. I over-estimated the size of the market for people studying advanced Latin and ancient Greek for pleasure. And after five years I sadly

took the dusty, yellowing editions of Plato's *Republic* and Ptolemy's *Geography* home.

8. **Making and selling T-shirts.** Looks easy: print up some T-shirts for six quid each and sell them for twenty. It isn't. What happens is that people wander in and say, 'I like that T-shirt in the window. Have you got it in XL/grey/white? You go downstairs and root through an enormous pile of T-shirts and are unable to find the precise combination of size and colour they require. So you go back upstairs, probably sweating, after ten minutes, and say, 'I'm so sorry, we don't have that one.' They leave without spending any money.

9. **Local book delivery by bicycle.** I thought this was a great wheeze. Locals could call our shop, buy a book over the phone, and we would cycle it round to their house. 'Quicker delivery than Amazon,' we could boast! We put Murray on a bicycle, took a picture, tweeted it, emailed it, did a press release. Nothing.

10. **Selling butterflies in cases.** Our friend Viktor Wynd suggested we sell his lovely cases of butterflies and stuffed owls in glass domes. We ordered them in, put them on the wall, priced them, photographed them, tweeted them, emailed them, did a press release. Again, nothing. In fact, I think we broke one so the whole exercise cost us money. Victoria and I took the broken one home and put it in the bathroom.

11. **Running a café.** Do you really want to serve two coffees to three yummy mummies who take up all the floor space, let their toddlers pull books off the shelves, then give you a fiver after an hour with an air that they are doing you a favour? Do you want to deal with whingeing customers and nutcases? No!

12. **Coding school.** This seemed like a good idea on paper: teach kids how to code. But other people are doing it better. We sold three places on our course. It was a waste of time.

Trying things out, failing, trying again, failing better, trying again ... this is an endless cycle which all businesses must suffer – including Google. What happened to Google Glass, for example, and how much money was spent on that piece of insanity? Google may be evil, but we bohemians can learn something from their example. Google have a policy of trying lots of things but not getting depressed when some things don't work. The mark of maturity is not to get over-attached to a particular idea but to let it go with a laugh at the right time.

You need to cultivate a Taoist attitude to your business, or businesses, and to your life. Again and again, when I talk to entrepreneurs, they agree that the endpoint is not a pile of cash but an enjoyable and satisfying every-day life. Dan Kieran of Unbound says that he was unemployable and needed a job. Starting Unbound with outside investment was the solution to this problem.

The first two or three years of the Idler Academy were

not happy-making for me – though, in many ways, they were satisfying – because I was spending too much time retailing, marketing and doing logistics and not enough time doing what I really enjoy, which is writing and editing. When Chris joined us, he got me back to commissioning and writing articles for the *Idler* website, and that was a great step forward. Now we have relaunched the *Idler* as a quarterly printing, and I am much happier.

As with negotiation, you need to know when to walk away from an idea, a project or cherished scheme. A very good idea is to keep a few projects on the go at any one time. Some are for money; some are not. Some will work; some will fail. Two of my gurus, Bill Drummond and Charles Handy, agree on this point. Go to Bill's website, penkiln-burn.com, and you'll see what I mean. At the time of writing, he has twelve crazy schemes. I'm sorry to repeat a cliché, but it's true: don't put all your eggs into one basket.

Don't try too hard. Do not waste your energy pushing in the wrong direction.

Find your way. Tune in with the logos. Don't waste energy doing stuff you are not suited to.

To that end, I would recommend making a simple list. Think back over the past few years and write down the things you have done or do which you enjoy or are comfortable with. Stick with those.

Simplify.

Abandon.

Give up.

Epilogue

Just as this book was going to press, I learned that we'd exceeded our funding target with our crowdfunding share sale, raising £150,000 for 13 per cent of the equity. This means our business is now valued at £1,150,000.

It happened in a strange way. Our campaign was on around £70,000. That was £50,000 short of our target, and we had two weeks to go. We'd had great publicity and lots of support, but somehow things had slowed down. I was out of my mind with stress. I had a drink with the editor of the *Evening Standard*'s Londoner's Diary and I could hardly talk, I was so worried. I knew that we'd be OK if we didn't reach our target, but that life would be more difficult. I think not knowing either way was also stressful.

We'd roped in our old friend James Pembroke, publisher of the *Oldie* magazine, to help guide the business and grow the magazine subscriptions. We had a meeting with James about our budgets and told him about our crowdfunding progress. He said, 'Tell you what, I might give Domino a call. By Domino he meant Dominic Armstrong, who I'd never heard of, but whose brother, the actor Alexander Armstrong, I used to know quite well.

Later that day, I received an email from Dominic, who since leaving university in the eighties, had made a fortune from setting up and selling a security firm, and was now living in Monaco. I pictured him sitting at an outdoor table in the sun with his laptop, a carafe of wine and a cigar before him, top three shirt buttons undone. 'I love the *Idler* and would love to invest. Would it be greedy to buy up all the remaining shares?'

Dominic did so, investing £50,000, and bringing us up to our target. This opened the floodgates for another few thousand. The company is now valued at over a million pounds.

So there it ended, my crowdfunding story. It was the most difficult thing I have ever done, and was made even more difficult by the fact that I was finishing off this book at the same time. I later heard from a start-up guy that his company put twenty people on their Crowcube campaign and they worked on it for six months. I did it practically alone. But the process itself – producing the financial models, business plan, snapshots, slide deck, video – helped us enormously to pin down what the business was really about and where it was going. But while you're actually doing the fundraising it is easy to take your eye off everyday sales, and our turnover actually dropped in the first half of 2016.

Londoner's Diary ran a lovely story which quoted Dominic as saying: 'The *Idler*'s philosophy is the perfect antidote to the noise, fury and vapidity of so much of life, a pure radio beacon in an age of static, a rose garden for the soul.'

We have 146 investors. It was lovely to see friends dropping in ten quid or a hundred quid. Most of the money, though, came from our top readers and customers, the people who really love what we do.

I feel that I have a family of shareholders who own the *Idler* with me and who I must now serve to the best of my ability. It is now a shared enterprise and feels not like a ruthless capitalist organization but like a co-operative which will spread joy but make a profit in the process.

I also now feel a greater sense of responsibility and accountability. In a sense I am now working for the shareholders and not for myself. In fact one night I woke up in a panic about this: gone are the days of sole proprietorship. I have duties.

So raising money by selling shares via a crowdfunding site can be done. But it is not a question of making a video, popping it online and waiting for the money to roll in. I would say that 90 per cent of the money came from our own efforts, and 10 per cent from investors that Crowdcube brought in. And bear in mind the following. 1. It will take you at least six months to prepare and 2. The money will come from your best customers and from the people to whom you go and personally present your idea. For us it was a hard slog, but well worth it in the end.

My final piece of advice is to get a good book-keeper and financial manager as early as you can. We had five years of false starts as far as that side of things went. Thanks to the above-mentioned James, we are now employing a financial manager who will do monthly accounts, chase invoices and make the payments.

Well, now it's time to get on with the work of creating and selling.

A Glossary of Terms

Upon entering the world of business from the more genteel one of writing and book publishing, I was shocked, horrified and amused by the number of absurd acronyms, business terms and piles of general corporate bullshit out there.

However, after hearing these terms being bandied around for a while, I realized that here was, very simply, a technical language which I really ought to study. When I worked at a skateboarding shop, I had to learn a whole new language: ollie kick-flips, decks, trucks, and so on. It is the same in carpentry, and it is the same in business. You need to sit down and learn the lingo.

The worst offenders are probably the geeks, the IT guys. They throw baffling terms around to the point where you suspect that they are trying to blind you with science. Here are a few recent examples from my own experience: 'The site looks to be whitelisted now; we have placed an html file in the root directory'; 'An update: the site works on our dev environment but when we pushed it to the live hosting the issue reappears but only for a specific version of Chrome'; 'It seems that the version is not respecting the session persistence on the load-balancer.'

Huh?

OK, it's easy to laugh. But really, it does not take long to learn such a language. I am starting to get fed up with people saying, 'I'm not tech savvy.' These days, it's a bit like saying, 'I can't drive', or 'I can't read'. Hopeless, really. If you want to be in business, then you need to gain a basic level of computer competency and knowledge of the terms of the craft you are studying. Even if you delegate this area to someone else, you need to have a basic understanding of it first. If you are not inclined to do a little bit of background study of this sort, then . . . erm . . . get a job.

Many of the acronyms emerge from the world of digital marketing – or DM, I should say. I have listed all the ones I have come across, and other business lingo, plus many more. Reading through them will reward patient study, even if you do consider half of the following to be BS of the highest order.

AIDA: Attention, Interest, Desire, Action. The
  four steps to making a sale.
Amortize: To write off the cost of an asset over
  time.
Angel investor: An angel is an individual investor
  who puts their own money into a small business
  in return for a share of ownership. Angels
  generally receive equity for their investment.
  They are hoping that an early investment will
  pay them back many times over but, also, they
  genuinely enjoy helping to build businesses.
Annuity: An annual payment that comes in without
  any effort, e.g. a pension or annual direct debit.
AOV: Average Order Value.
API: Application Program Interface.

Appraisal: Term for an annual interview with a staff member about how they're getting on. John Brown says appraisals are important and recommends that both parties should produce a list of ten points, both good and bad.

ATL: Above The Line. Refers to marketing and advertising in very visible media like TV and newspapers.

B2B: Business to Business. Refers to a business whose customer or clients are other businesses and not everyday consumers.

B2C: Business to Consumer. A business that sells direct to consumers, e.g. Argos.

Balance sheet: The page in your accounts that lists your assets and liabilities, i.e. how much you own and are owed versus how much you owe.

Brand: A recognizable logo or company name. Brands also have something called 'values', believe it or not. Examples of brand values may include things like youth, vitality, experimentation and freedom. I've always thought that it would be fun to create a new brand with values like hatred, cynicism and fear, but I'm not sure how that would go down in business circles. Oh, hang on – *Vice* and the *Daily Mail* have already done it.

CMS: Content Management System.

Controlling interest: Owning more than 50 per cent of the shares of a company, and therefore having the power in decision-making.

CRM: Customer Relationship Management.

CTA: Call To Action.

Current assets: A company's cash or assets which could be converted into cash within one year.

Customer service: If you are dealing with consumers every day, you have to get good at dealing with complaints pretty smartish. Complaints are your friends!

CX: Customer Experience.

Deck: This refers to a presentation that you have created on PowerPoint or Keynote. It is short for 'a deck of slides' (like a deck of cards, geddit?).

Dividend: A portion of profits paid by a company to its shareholders.

DNS: Domain Name System.

End consumer or end user: The customer who buys your product or service.

Fixed assets: Machinery, property, furniture, coffee machines, other companies, cars – in fact, anything owned by a business.

Fixed costs: The overheads you have to pay whether you get an order or not. Things like wages, office costs, rent, business rates, electricity and gas, insurance, technical support. A common term for the same thing is 'overheads'. You need to make a list of these in order to know the minimum amount of business you need to do in order to keep the show on the road.

FMCG: Fast-Moving Consumer Goods. The kind of stuff Amazon sells. Pile it high, sell it cheap.

Footfall: The number of people passing your place of business. We eventually gave up our first retail outlet because of lack of footfall.

Fulfilment: The process of getting the customer's order to them. When we get an order, we fulfil it either through mail order or through digital means.

GA: Google Analytics.

Goodwill: The intangible and unmeasurable assets of a company, things like brand value, intellectual property, relationships. Goodwill can be under- or over-valued: that is a question for debate.

Greyhair: A board director hired by a young start-up who is older and more experienced in business than the founders. The idea is that the presence of the greyhair will assure investors that the proposition is trustworthy.

Gross profit margin: This is what is left from each sale after the cost of the goods has been accounted for. For example, a pizza sells for £10 and its ingredients cost £1; gross profit margin is 90 per cent.

Hand selling: A term used by bookshops for the process of recommending particular books to a customer, having listened to their preferences or needs.

High net worth: Rich, used in phrases such as 'She is a high-net-worth individual.' You often hear of business people targeting this group, in a rather distasteful fashion.

HIPPO: HIghest Paid Person's Opinion.

HR: Human Resources.

HTML: HyperText Mark-up Language.

Insolvency: Not having enough assets or cash to pay what you owe. Companies are not supposed to trade when they are insolvent, but many clearly do.

Intrapreneur: An individual who works on the staff in a big company but brings in an entrepreneurial way of thinking by developing new ideas.

IP: Intellectual Property (e.g. an idea).

IPO: Initial Public Offering. This is when a company raises money by selling shares on the stock exchange.

Kaizen: Japanese for 'improvement'. This is the process of making small improvements to your business every day. This process helps you to welcome customer complaints as useful feedback which will make you money one day, rather than a source of stress.

KPI: Key Performance Indicator. Any method of your choice to measure the success of your venture, e.g. earnings, number of website visitors, targets.

Lifestyle business: The contemporary term for 'cottage industry'. A small business, often run from home, which leaves the owner plenty of time for other areas of life, such as spending it with family or friends, and which may not have ambitious plans for growth.

Limited liability: If a limited-liability company goes bust, the shareholders will lose their shares but not any other assets which they may own.

Low-hanging fruit: Easy and visible sales or opportunities to grab.

MVP: Minimum Viable Product. This is a term for testing your market. Just ship something, is the idea. Get something out there and see how it goes.

P&L: Profit and Loss spreadsheet.

Plug-in: A bit of software that bolts on to the main program and adds a certain feature.

POS: Point Of Sale. In a bookshop, for example, this is the area around the till.

Positive free cashflow: This essentially means that your bank account is in the black and you are no longer running a Ponzi scheme, i.e. paying for previous supplies with the payments from new ones. Cash inflows are higher than cash outflows. The money you have left once you have paid all your bills is positive free cash flow. Some investors have no interest in positive free cashflow situations: for example, Etsy loses millions of dollars every year but its shares are trading well on the stock exchange.

PPC: Pay Per Click: This is what happens if you set up an ad with Google, that is, you pay a certain amount of money each time someone clicks on your ad. In our experience it is a total waste of money, the only people who benefit being the agency who took your money and, of course, Google.

Q1, Q2, Q3, Q4: Refers to the first, second, third and fourth quarter of the year.

ROI: Return On Investment.

SEM: Search Engine Marketing.

SEO: Search Engine Optimization. The process whereby you attempt to ensure that your business appears on the front page of search engines. In my experience, it is best ignored in favour of national press, continually releasing new products and publishing articles. One piece in the *Daily Telegraph* or the *Guardian* will do more for your SEO than a million tweets.

SSL: Secure Sockets Layer. This is something to do with your email settings and is guaranteed to drive you insane.

Subscription: A regular payment made by a customer in return for the regular fulfilment of a service or product. A subscription-based service could be an excellent business model for a small entrepreneur without funding.

SUS: Sexy Up-Shift. This refers to the process by which the übergeeks take a previously unsexy industry – lonely hearts, minicabs, mail order, letting out your spare room, car-boot sales, hiring a cleaner – and make it modern and groovy, e.g. Tinder, Uber, Amazon, Airbnb, eBay and TaskRabbit. Another term for it is 'disruption'.

Sweat the asset: Get the most out of the things you own or rent. For example, when renting a shop, you really ought to 'sweat the asset' by keeping it open or having it used as many hours in the week as you possibly can. Our shop often sat empty for three or four days a week – a waste of rent money.

TLA: Three-Letter Acronym. (OK, I made that one up.)

Top Line Summary: A brief synopsis of a meeting or business decision given to time-strapped top brass who can't be bothered to read the whole document.

UGC: User-Generated Content. The übergeeks out there have made vast fortunes by tricking users into giving them free entertainment, against which they sell advertising, by claiming that they are providing an outlet for creativity.

URL: Uniform Resource Locator. A web address; the thing that starts http://

User: Someone who has signed up to use your website. What used to be called a customer.

USP: Unique Selling Proposition. This is something that your product or service can offer which no one else can.

UTS: User Too Stupid. A little geek joke. This TLA is used when a customer emails to say

'Your system doesn't work!' but in fact is not technologically literate enough to use it. One geek says to another, 'I think this is a UTS issue.'

Venture capitalist: Someone who works for a company which uses other people's money to invest in business in search of high returns. As a direct result of this set-up, enormous pressure can be put on entrepreneurs. Probably best avoided unless you really, really want a yacht and a butler.

WTP: What's The Point. The moment you realize you are working sixteen hours a day to create income which goes to other people and never to you: staff, landlord, council, tax office and suppliers.

WYSIWYG: What You See Is What You Get.

YCPT: You Can't Polish a Turd. A term used when the directors of a business finally recognize that no one is going to buy their crap product, no matter how much marketing they do.

YTD: Year To Date.

Further Reading

To prepare this book, and to try to help me run my own business in a more enjoyable and efficient fashion, I sat down and read a pile of business books. Most of those below are mentioned in the text. The principle is to read these guides, but also to read the classic works of philosophy, or books about classic philosophy.

In general, I prefer reading books that have been recommended by others to Googling what I want. Recommendations on the Web are patchy and often dated. You have no real idea whether the information you are reading is of good quality or not. Furthermore, half of these so-called 'resource' websites are in fact just ads for a book or a course.

That's why I have not bothered to provide a list of websites. In the UK, my advice would be to join the Federation of Small Businesses and use their advice lines. They have lawyers and accountants who will talk to members for free. I've also noticed that the stuff put online by HMRC these days isn't half bad.

Carnegie, Dale, *How to Win Friends and Influence People* (Vermilion). Old but still relevant and a classic, with some great lists of what to do.
Dennis, Felix, *How to Get Rich* (Ebury Press). Great fun and good advice from the ultimate bohemian businessman.

Drummond, Bill, *The Manual*. Out of print, but a great guide to running a creative business.

Epictetus, *Discourses, Fragments, Handbook* (Oxford's World Classics). Stoic philosophy.

Evans, Jules, *Philosophy for Life and Other Dangerous Situations* (Ebury Press). A Stoic primer for the modern age.

The FT Guide to Writing a Business Plan (FT Publishing). Boring but useful to have by the bedside.

Gallo, Hilary, *The Power of Soft* (Ebury Press). Great advice on negotiation from the Zen master.

Handy, Charles, *The Second Curve* (Random House). How to start planning a new stage of life or business before the existing one goes into decline. The *Idler*'s favourite management guru.

Hodgkinson, Tom, *How to be Free* (Penguin). My second book is a cheering collection of essays on how to develop mental liberation.

Johnson, Luke, *Start It Up* (Portfolio Penguin). Useful tips from someone who knows what he is talking about.

Lott, Tim, *The Idler Guide to Eastern Philosophy* (Idler Press). Handy guide to the key concepts behind Zen, Taoism and Buddhism.

Lymer, Andy, *Teach Yourself Small Business Accounting* (Teach Yourself). A must-have, even if you hire a book-keeper.

Marcus Aurelius, *Meditations* (Penguin Classics). Stoic philosophy.

Murningham, Keith, *Do Nothing: How to Stop Overmanaging and Become a Great Leader* (Penguin Portfolio). This is my favourite management book. He tells you to trust your staff more in order that you may do less and less until one day, you do precisely nothing. That is the Zen-like aim.

Reed, James, *Why You?: 101 Interview Questions You'll Never Fear Again* (Portfolio Penguin). A brilliant guide from someone who really does know what he is talking about when it comes to staff and people.

Ries, Eric, *The Lean Startup* (Portfolio Penguin). On how to experiment with new products.

Rousseau, Jean-Jacques, *Reveries of a Solitary Walker* (Penguin Classics). A book for your idle time.

Scott, James C., *Two Cheers for Anarchism* (Princeton University Press). A superb defence of anarchism by a distinguished Yale professor. Scott defends the small businesspeople as the true anarchists and also celebrates the spirit of revolt.

Seneca, *Letters from a Stoic* (Penguin Classics). Stoic philosophy.

Vernon, Mark, *The Idler Guide to Ancient Philosophy* (Idler Press). Readable account of the key philosophies of ancient Athens, from Stoicism to Epicureanism.

Watts, Alan, *The Wisdom of Insecurity* (Rider). Why it is foolish to cling too tightly to your dreams.

Wickman, Gino, *Traction: Get a Grip on Your Business* (BenBella Books). Useful hints and tips on creating systems that work.

Xenophon, *The Oeconomicus* (Loeb). The original self-help book. Advice on estate management.

Acknowledgements

Thanks to Simon Prosser for suggesting I write this. And to . . . the most excellent Portfolio editors, Zoe Bohm and Fred Baty, for taking the stream-of-consciousness rant of my first draft and helping me to turn it into something vaguely coherent. To Sarah Day for polishing it up. To Ellie Smith for calmly dealing with last-minute changes. To Cat Ledger, my agent, for making sure I get paid, and for being such a joy in general. To John Brown, who kindly allowed me to weave his top-ten business tips into the text. To James Pembroke, John Lloyd, Charles Handy, Ed Jenne, Christian Dangerfield, John Mitchinson, Emma Thompson, Robin Birley, Dan Kieran, Lucy Birley and all our Crowdcube investors for supporting my doings with advice, money or good cheer. To Simone and Alan from Clever Boxer. To Luke Johnson, Serena Rees and James Reed for giving talks. To all our tutors at the Idler Academy who are such fun to work with. To all *Idler* contributors. To Julian Mash and Roberta McCaughan for working with me. To our customers and readers all over the world for spending money with us. But most of all to Victoria Hull for her business and creative brilliance and for coping with me on a day-to-day basis.